WE BELIEVE

An interpretation of the 1963 Mennonite Confession
of Faith for the younger generation

by Paul Erb

HERALD PRESS, Scottdale, Pennsylvania

Preface

What do I believe? And why do I believe it? These questions every Christian should be able to answer. As soon as a person is old enough to have a Christian faith, he is also old enough to grow in an understanding of his faith.

The purpose of this booklet is to help young Christians to believe more intelligently and to be able to answer questions concerning their faith. Questions have been added to each section for purposes of private study or for use in Sunday school classes or youth groups.

This material was first published in 1967 as a series of articles in *Youth's Christian Companion*. There have been calls for its availability in this more permanent form.

The chapters are based on the twenty articles of the *Mennonite Confession of Faith* adopted by Mennonite General Conference in 1963. See page 91 for the full *Mennonite Confession of Faith*. There is also a shorter form, the various sections of which are quoted at the beginning of the chapters of this booklet. The text is something of a commentary on this shorter Confession of Faith, also showing what the various articles mean for daily living. For Christians should behave their faith as well as believe it.

It is the author's prayer that this booklet may find further usefulness in teaching our young people, and possibly older ones too, the fuller meaning of what they have accepted as truth.

Paul Erb

We Believe

1. GOD IS

We believe in one God eternally existing as Father, Son, and Holy Spirit.

God is. Most people ought to be able to go along with that. How else can we explain what we see all about us? A solar system that runs with split-second precision; physical laws which scientists keep discovering, but which they cannot create; a fine balance between the various life-forms and the elements needed to sustain them. To say that these things just happened would be naive.

No, a watch argues the existence of a watch-maker. A fence on the Western plains argues a fence-maker, even though there is not another sign of human habitation around. How could there be a pattern without a pattern-maker, a design without a designer, a creation that makes sense without an intelligent Maker who put sense into it?

Modern science does not make God unnecessary; it

7

simply keeps making Him more wonderful. Science does not prove there is a God. For God is above and before all that He has made, else He is only a part of creation —of somebody else's creation. We do not demonstrate God through science; a God that you could fix your telescope upon or spot under your microscope would not be God.

No, the more we learn in our scientific age, the greater God becomes, the more credible it is that Somebody must have made the universe in which we find ourselves, and whose marvels scientists keep discovering and describing. The heavens and the atoms declare Him. If we knew only science, we would have to call God the Great Probable.

BUT THIS Great Hypothesis of science, whom the Greeks worshiped as the Unknown God, has revealed Himself to us. "The Word of the Lord" came to a whole succession of prophets and apostles, and these words of God are collected in the Bible, which we can read.

He revealed Himself also in a person who walked our earth almost two thousand years ago and called Himself the Son of God. He accepted worship as God. His claims were made valid by a succession of observable signs, climaxed in His resurrection from the dead. Those who lived with Him were convinced by His words and deeds and by the unique force of His personality that He came from the Father God, as He claimed.

How explain the Bible and Jesus without believing that there is a God?

But, some say, Jesus lived a long time ago, and the Bible is an ancient Book. Is God still alive and working today? Hundreds of thousands testify that He is.

The Bible speaks of the Spirit of God, sent by the Father and the Son to do the continuing work of God in the world. He speaks to us in our inmost being. He searches our hearts and convinces us that we are sinners. He guides us daily, even in small details of our lives. He gives us power to overcome the sin in our natures and to do the work to which God has called us.

We believe in God because in our spirits we can communicate with Him. Someone told Stuart Hamblen, the Christian cowboy songwriter, that God is dead. Stuart replied, "Buddy, you're wrong; I just finished talking to Him." Many people experience reality in talking with God. God hears and answers their prayers.

This God to whom we speak and who speaks to us is beyond mere laboratory demonstration. He is not contrary to science: He is greater than science, and no less real because He is beyond our full comprehension.

THE GOD some people say they cannot believe in is not the God the Bible describes. As children we may have built a mental image of a big man with white hair and piercing eyes, sitting on a throne surrounded by fleecy clouds. This God, out there somewhere, no longer makes sense to us. This is good, for we ought to grow up. The Bible does not tell us of such a God, the "man upstairs."

God is spirit; He has no physical form limited, however big, to some one place. He is everywhere at the same time. He is the eternal God, who had no beginning and will have no end. We cannot understand this, for it is beyond anything we have experienced. It simply shows that God is greater than we are; He is not just one of ourselves.

The Bible pictures God as all-knowing and all-powerful, which is the reason some people are afraid of Him. But He also loves; this is at the heart of His nature. And His love is toward us; it includes all the world. This attracts us to Him.

For discussion:

1. In what ways does science help or hinder your understanding of God?
2. Why do you think Jesus came from God?
3. How do you know God is alive today?
4. Describe God as you understand Him; how do you feel about God?

For your notebook:

Initiate conversations about God with five persons during the next week. Talk with different types of persons such as a classmate who considers himself an involved Christian, a classmate who questions God, a teacher, an older Christian friend, a person whom you just happen to meet. Find out what each one thinks about God. Don't write anything while you talk but immediately following each conversation, jot down several phrases to help you remember your discussion. After finishing all five, summarize your conversations in a one-page essay.

2. GOD SPEAKS

We believe that God has revealed Himself in the Scriptures of the Old and New Testaments, the inspired Word of God, and supremely in His Son, the Lord Jesus Christ.

One of the Old Testament prophets complains about man-made idols, that they are dumb; they cannot speak. Habakkuk 2:18, 19. How ridiculous, he says, to expect a wooden carving or a dumb stone, in which there is no breath at all, to say anything! "Can this give revelation?" he asks.

Of course it cannot; therefore it is no god. A god who exists, who has intelligence and power, may be expected to say something. Communication is a chief evidence of being and thinking. If God is God, He ought to have spoken.

God ought to be able to communicate. And He is able. He has spoken. God spoke to Abraham, Isaac, and Jacob.

The "Word of the Lord" came to Moses, to David, and to a long line of prophets. These men told to others what the Lord told to them. And in many cases they wrote it down, so that this Word of the Lord could come to generations yet unborn.

And so there gradually grew the collection of books which we call the Old Testament: history, laws, poetry, proverbs, prophecy. The Old Testament claims again and again that in these books we are given, not the thoughts of men, but a message from our God.

But God has spoken to us also in Jesus His Son. "In many and various ways God spoke of old to our fathers by the prophets; but in these last days he has spoken to us by a Son" (Hebrews 1:1, 2). This Jesus called the Old Testament the Word of God. But He was also Himself the Word of God. In His person, His words, and His work Jesus revealed His Father unto men.

After the resurrection of Jesus, the apostles became the reliable witnesses to the words and deeds of Christ. The message of salvation which they preached was the "word of God." This message was based on the. Old Testament, but also on their oral testimony that the Scriptures centered in the Christ they had seen and heard.

But since these eyewitnesses would not always be here, their spoken testimony was gradually put into writing. The apostles—Paul, Peter, John, James, Jude, and whichever one it was that wrote *Hebrews*—wrote letters to the Christians at various places. The letters, that part of the New Testament which we call epistles, further explain the message which the apostles preached. They give directions for the problems which the Christians faced. No doubt some of them were circulated from church to church. Through them the Holy Spirit continued to teach.

THE STORY of the life and the teachings of Jesus was written in a new kind of literature called a Gospel. Based on a great deal of oral material four of these Gospels were written. *Matthew* was a compilation representing the viewpoint of the Jewish Christians. *Mark* wrote a summary of Peter's teaching about Jesus. *Luke* put into his book the Gospel which Paul preached. And last of all *John*, in a meditative style, interprets the Gospel from the spiritual viewpoint of Christian believers.

Jesus had told His disciples that the Spirit would bring back to their memories these things concerning Him. In the four Gospels we have this Spirit-directed recollection.

To the Epistles and the Gospels were added a history, *Acts*, and a prophecy, *Revelation*.

When the apostles died, the writings which they had given the churches were gradually collected into an approved list which the churches recognized as the continuing Word of God to them. We call this collection today *The New Testament*.

WE BELIEVE that God speaks to us, even today, through His Son. The Bible, in both Testaments, witnesses concerning Him.

Through the Bible God tells us many things we could not know of ourselves: where we came from, where we are going, how to behave while here, and how to make life meaningful and worthwhile. But primarily God's Word was written and preserved to bring us into a living relationship with the saving Christ. And to know Him is to know God.

13

Our God is not a dumb image that we have created. No, He has spoken and He speaks today through the record He has given us of His Son. He speaks; if we are wise, we will listen.

For discussion:

1. In what ways does God speak to men?

2. Describe what the Bible is. Explain what each of the Testaments is about.

3. What are the particular characteristics of the first four books of the New Testament? What is the overall purpose of the four Gospels?

4. Why did God provide a Bible?

For your notebook:

Prepare a one-page report on the general idea of "revelation" (not the New Testament book). Compare the definitions given in a regular dictionary and in a Bible dictionary. Check the index to J. C. Wenger's *Introduction to Theology.* Ask an older Christian (like your parents, youth sponsor, or pastor) to explain some of the things about revelation you find hard to understand.

3. GOD MADE

We believe that in the beginning God created all things by His Son. He made man in the divine image, with free will, moral character, and a spiritual nature.

Did you ever hear of a self-made man? Isn't any man who claims to be self-made a joke? Everybody knows what such a man owes to his father's money, his mother's family connections, the good teachers he had, the people who wrote the books he read, the social setting which gave him his opportunities.

There never was a self-made man. Not even Adam. The psalmist sang,

> "Know that the Lord is God!
>   It is he that made us,
>   And we are his."

Man comes from God.

Neither is there a self-made earth. Created man lives in a created world. Our earth is a part of a created universe. Astronomers talk about young suns and dying suns. Nature is a continuing process, moving from beginnings toward ends. Science is the description of that process.

But it is only from the Bible that we can learn what the real beginning was. That biblical word is, "In the beginning God created the heaven and the earth" (Genesis 1:1). The Bible is clear that everything which exists is from God; everything depends on Him. This is the ground truth of the Christian religion.

To believe this is not to disbelieve science. Science is gradually telling us the *what* and the *how* of the physical universe. It does not attempt to give us the *who* and the *why*. This we get from religion; our religion gets it from the Bible. There is no contradiction between the two. James Dana, a Christian and one of the greatest geologists of the last century, said, "There can be no real conflict between the two books of the Great Author." The book of nature and the Word of God help each other to tell the full story.

The Bible tells us that God created, but it does not tell us when or how. It is not the purpose of the Bible to serve as a science textbook. The only word in Genesis 1 on the when is, "In the beginning." All the time records of geology are on this side of that beginning.

And on the how Genesis tells us only that the creation was orderly, systematic, and progressive. The forms of life are from the more simple to the more complex, with man as the latest and highest. Within that outline science finds its facts.

When science and the Bible seem to disagree, it may be either that the science is only unproved theory, or that the Bible is misinterpreted. Some people believe

16

in evolution because they want to rather than because the facts are clear.

And some people believe the date of creation is 4004 B.C. because a seventeenth-century Irish archbishop got this date written into the margin of the Bible, and not because the Bible itself gives a date for this far-off event.

BECAUSE GOD is the Creator, it is only He who is to be worshiped. It is wrong to make a god out of something that God has made. We worship only Him who is behind all other causes, the Being beyond all being. Why should we worship the sun instead of the Creator of the sun?

Our bodies are similar in many ways to the bodies of other mammals. But we do not believe that man is only the most highly evolved mammal. We believe that God created man "in his image." What does that mean?

It does not mean that we have bodies like God's. For God is spirit, and He has no material body.

We are in His image because He made us like Himself in certain ways. Not in all ways, for then we would be God; the creature would have become the Creator.

He gave us minds to think. When Kepler, the astronomer, discovered some laws which govern the movement of planets, he exclaimed in awe, "I am thinking God's thoughts after Him." Engineering skill which thrusts rockets into space is different in its nature from the instincts which guide the migration of birds.

Man can say, "I will" or "I won't." In this power of choice he is like God.

Man has a sense that "I ought to do this" and "I ought not to do this." In his moral nature he is like God.

Man is a spirit who lives in a body, and will live eter-

17

nally. In this too he is like God.

God is a Maker. Man is His creature, responsible to his Maker.

For discussion:

1. What is science?
2. What is the ground truth of the Christian religion?
3. How would you relate science and Christian faith?
4. Why should men worship God?

For your notebook:

The Book of Genesis reports that God made man in His own image. From the earliest times men have been trying to understand what is involved in being created in the image of God. The matter is not simple. Interview two ministers in your community to get their opinions on the matter. Explain that you are studying the doctrines of your church and you would like their help. Take notes as the men talk with you. On the basis of these interviews, combined with your own personal research, write a 500-word essay on "What It Means to Be Made in God's Image."

4. WE ARE SINNERS

We believe that man fell into sin, bringing depravity and death upon the race; that as sinner, man is self-centered and self-willed, unwilling and unable to break with sin.

Sobbing repentantly, a twelve-year-old girl asked her father, "What makes me act like that?" *That* was an angry outbreak of words against her mother. "It's because you are my daughter," the father replied. He explained that he too had a hot temper, which, when he was a child, broke out into uncontrolled tantrums.

We inherit from our parents a sinful, depraved nature. You do not remember, do you, the first time you ever did something that you knew was wrong? You may remember when you first realized that you had sinned. For most of us, however, that realization came gradually.

As tiny tots we screamed angrily when we couldn't

have our way. We selfishly snatched the toys from our playmates. We stole cookies and candy, and tried to lie out of it.

BUT THESE sins—surely they were that—did not bother us. We were too young to know that we were doing anything wrong. We only sensed that our parents disapproved. We were sinners, all right, but we didn't know it. And God did not hold us responsible, because we were children, not knowing right from wrong. And as innocent children we belonged to God.

Then gradually, out of this innocence, we knew that we were sinners. No one needed to tell us; we just knew it. It wasn't that we were wicked today; we became aware that we had been wicked all along. We knew now that we were accountable to God for the things we did. We had become responsible.

C. H. Spurgeon, the great English preacher, beginning at the age of ten was convicted of sin. "Those who examined my life would not have seen any extraordinary sin, yet as I looked upon *myself*, I saw outrageous sin against God. Of a sudden I met Moses, carrying the law—God's Ten Words—and as I read them, they all seemed to join in condemning me in the sight of the thrice holy Jehovah."

The Bible says that all men are sinners:

"There is no man who does not sin" (1 Kings 8:46).

"They have all gone astray" (Psalm 14:3).

"We have turned every one to his own way" (Isaiah 53:6).

"The heart is deceitful . . . and desperately corrupt" (Jeremiah 17:9).

"All have sinned" (Romans 3:23).

20

We must all say as Peter said to Jesus, "I am a sinful man."

PREACHERS DID NOT invent this idea. We see evidences of it all around us, in every newspaper. Most laws exist because people cannot settle their disputes honestly and unselfishly. We need contracts because our promises are not enough. We need locks and keys because people steal.

Somebody at the door of the public library must inspect the books you carry out. The teacher guards against cheating on examination day. Policemen must patrol our streets. It is dangerous to walk alone in the dark. We need protection from one another. What a sorry fix our depraved natures have got us into!

But it isn't the other person's sins that bother us most. It is our own. Try as we will, we come short of our ideals. Something within us makes us chafe at restraints and challenge the laws of parents, of school, of church, of God. We think thoughts that are impure and feel impulses which, if followed, would land us in jail.

We try desperately to give others the impression that we are something different from what we know we are. We look in the mirror and say, *You thief! You cheat! You murderer! You fornicator! You liar! You snob! You self-worshiper!* Oh, we may not be all that, but we know the threat of it all is within us.

And of ourselves we don't know what to do about it. We are slaves to a tyrant malady that we can't get rid of. It's as if we had inherited a loathsome disease.

THE WORST OF it is that our sins create a barrier between us and God. God is in a mist that we can't get through. We are at the same time strangers to God and afraid of Him.

Paul explains in Romans 5 that it was the sin of Adam that plunged the human race into this disaster of depravity. But the guilt we bear is our own, for we have opened our hearts to evil, and shut them against the good.

Unless God reaches down to save us, we have no hope.

For discussion:

1. Where does sin come from?
2. How do you know there is sin in the world?
3. When did you discover sin in your own experience?
4. What really is sin? (A Bible concordance to check ways in which the word is used may give you some clues.)

For your notebook:

Save your daily newspaper for one week and then clip items which illustrate how sin affects our world. Select photos, news stories, advertisements, and headlines as materials for pasting up a poster or collage. Use several sheets in your notebook (or scotch-tape two or more sheets together to form a pullout). After the exercise, write down your feelings about sin; you may want to express your feelings in a poem or a song, rather than in straight writing.

5. WE NEED A SAVIOR

We believe that there is one Mediator between God and men, the Man Christ Jesus, who died to redeem us from sin and arose for our justification.

Martin Luther one day stood before a picture of Christ upon the cross. Tears filled his eyes as he murmured, "For me! For me!" What did he mean?

Last week's meditation in this series closed with the words, "Unless God reaches down to save us, we have no hope." The sin of our nature, and the sins we have committed, have built a wall of separation between us and God. Our consciences condemn us. We are ashamed and confused. We feel guilty, but are helpless to do anything about it. The Bible says we are like lost sheep, unable to find our way home.

The good news is that God has reached down to meet our need. He has not turned from us in disgust and anger because of what we have done. He has not doomed us to the pain of exile from Him.

What God did was to send His Son into the world to be the cure for our lostness. Jesus said when He was here, "The Son of Man is come to seek and save the lost." He is the Good Shepherd who finds the lost sheep and brings it home. He is the Mediator who stands between God and the sinner to make peace between them. He is the Lamb of God, offered as a sacrifice to make atonement for sin.

That figure of the sacrificial animal, killed and offered to secure release from guilt, made sense to the people of Jesus' day. Through the years they had brought many gallons of blood from their calves and lambs and kids, that their sins might be forgiven. Without the shedding of blood, they knew, there could be no peace in their hearts. This was the way God had commanded.

But all these sacrifices could stop when the Son of God died upon the cross. For He was offered once to bear the sins of many. This is what John the Baptist meant when he pointed to Jesus and said, "Behold, the Lamb of God, who takes away the sin of the world!" This is the death and sacrifice that is effective once and for all.

That is the reason you see crosses on churches and elsewhere as the distinctive symbol of the Christian faith. Death on a Roman cross was a terrible disgrace. But because of what Jesus accomplished on the cross, it has become a symbol of honor, even of adoration. We sing,

In the cross of Christ I glory.

The central figure of the Bible is Christ, and the central event of Christ's ministry is His death on the cross. More than one third of the four Gospels is used to report the last week of His life.

And the rest of the New Testament witnesses to the supreme importance of what was done at the cross. Here Jesus, as a priest, without any sin of His own, offered Himself for our sins. Here He was made sin, counted as a sinner, in order that we might be made righteous.

Through His death He defeated the devil and all his works. Here He tasted death for every man. He bore our sins in His body on the tree. By His wounds we have been healed. He was put to death on account of our trespasses. He reconciled God and man, making peace by the blood of His cross.

Here He demonstrated God's love, which was His own: Paul says Christ loved him and gave Himself for him. And in Revelation the hosts worship a Lamb that had been slain.

In the beautiful hymn about the green hill far away Mrs. Cecil F. Alexander sings:

We believe it was for us
   He hung and suffered there.

It was indeed, and as we look to Him there in faith, we know that in Him the troubled sinner has found the Savior he needs. He has lost his burden of guilt, his bondage to sin, and the discord that made him afraid of God.

Menno Simons once wrote to a woman who had a troubled conscience because of her many faults. He said, "In and through Christ you are justified and pleasing to God, and accepted in eternal grace as a daughter and child. . . . His precious blood alone is your cleansing; His righteousness, your piety; His death, your life. . . . For He is the forgiveness of all your sin; His bloody wounds are your reconciliation."

For discussion:

1. What separates men from God?
2. How can men and God get together?
3. Why is the cross a distinctive symbol of the Christian faith?
4. What was the central event of Christ's life on earth?

For your notebook:

Amid a culture which emphasizes talk and busyness, it is usual for people, particularly men, not to express their feelings. But your understanding of Christ's cross in relation to you demands emotional as well as intellectual involvement. Allow yourself 60 minutes of uninterrupted quiet to record your feelings about the cross. You may want to sketch or draw with crayons or felt markers your personal response to the cross or you may want to express yourself in a poem or in a song.

6. CHRIST SAVES US

We believe that salvation is by grace through faith in Christ, a free gift bestowed by God on those who repent and believe.

One day when I was about fifteen I was going about my chores in our dairy barn. The words of a Bible verse I had just memorized were running through my mind: "For the wages of sin is death; but the gift of God is eternal life through Jesus Christ our Lord" (Romans 6:23).

Suddenly the meaning of that verse burst upon me. I saw in the first clause that the sinner is paid for his sin; and that his wage is death. What he gets, he deserves, for he worked for it. The logical consequence of sin is death—physical death, spiritual death, the death of eternal separation from God.

The second half of the verse is in contrast to the first.

The one who gets life through Christ gets a gift. He does not deserve this gift, for he is a sinner. But he receives something beyond his deserving. It is by grace that he receives life.

I saw the difference between wages and a gift, and it was clear as day to me that the salvation I had received through Christ was a gift, and not wages. If I had got what I deserved, it would have been, not life, but death. I could hardly wait until the next Wednesday evening prayer meeting to give my testimony of the great truth God had showed to me.

SALVATION BY grace is a gift; salvation by something in ourselves is wages. Salvation from the guilt and bondage of sin comes by faith, not by trying. And the faith is in Christ, not in ourselves and anything we can do; nor in other people, and anything they can do for us.

A lady on the train, when I asked her whether she was a Christian, exclaimed, "Oh, yes. My father was a preacher and my two grandfathers were preachers. Religion just runs in our family." She seemed to be putting her trust in her ancestry, for she said nothing about Christ. She forgot, if she ever knew, that all Adam's children are sinners.

When I asked a barber whether he was saved, he answered, "I pay the priest to see about that." Instead of looking to Christ, he was trusting in a man, and he thought his money could buy all the soul insurance he needed. The Bible says we are not saved by gold or silver. Not even by greenbacks and checks.

One woman wished that her husband could be baptized, so that he would be sure to be saved. That is like the people of Paul's day who thought they could be saved by being circumcised and offering sacrifices and observing a thousand and one regulations about the Sabbath.

One young man knew he was a Christian because he wore a certain kind of coat. Or a girl may think she earns salvation by wearing a prayer covering. Some try to gain salvation by going to church and paying their dues and attending communion or mass. Getting salvation by doing such things would be earning a wage, not receiving a gift.

Some of us pride ourselves that we haven't done anything very bad. We aren't murderers or thieves, prostitutes, or alcoholics. We think such people are the ones who really need a Savior. If we truly saw our own sin in comparison with God's requirement, instead of with other people's sins, we would understand that a man on Mt. Everest is practically as far away from the stars as one at the bottom of a mine shaft far below sea level.

With a Jewish friend I attended a Day of Atonement service. He asked what I thought of it. I told him I had heard a lot of confession of sin, but where was the atonement? He told me that it is in the good things that we do—our charities and benevolences. He was buying his salvation, he thought. If he did more good than bad, the balance would be in his favor.

The New Testament tells, "By grace are ye saved through faith; and that not of yourselves: it is the gift of God: not of works, lest any man should boast." The merit lies in Christ, not in us. To seek to secure God's favor by our own efforts is an insult to Jesus Christ. For that says He came to earth in vain, that He need not have died upon the cross, that we can get along without Him.

TO BELIEVE IN Christ is to put our dependence upon

Him. Without faith we cannot be saved. Faith is as necessary as the hand that takes the gift, as the mouth that eats the offered food. This we can and must do. But this is not earning anything. It is receiving the greatest gift in the world from the greatest Giver of all.

For discussion:

1. Why did Christ die?

2. Paraphrase Romans 6:23 in your own words.

3. Why is the fact of salvation as a gift hard for so many people to understand?

4. What is faith?

For your notebook:

Christian faith means that a man believes, and that he practices what he believes. Explain your understanding of "faith" in a short essay. Use some resources from your home, church, or pastor's library to give you background. It may also be helpful to check with some persons to clarify some of the things which you do not understand in the books which you consult. Include your personal ideas as well as what you read and hear from others.

7. THE SPIRIT LIVES IN US

We believe that the Holy Spirit convicts of sin, effects the new birth, gives guidance in life, empowers for service, and enables perseverance in faith and holiness.

Do you believe in spirits? The writers of the New Testament did. The Holy Spirit is spoken of in all the New Testament books except three very brief ones— Philemon, 2 John, and 3 John. Paul in his epistles refers to the Spirit about 120 times. Belief in this Holy Spirit of God is really a very important part of the Christian faith.

The Bible speaks of God as three persons: Father, Son and Spirit. Not three Gods—there is *one* God—but God in a threefold functioning. God the Father is the Source of all things. God the Son is the Revealer and Redeemer. God the Spirit is the Executive, doing the work of God. The Bible does not explain the Trinity; it simply shows God functioning in these three persons.

THROUGH THE WORK of the Holy Spirit God comes into our daily experience. It is the Spirit who is with us wherever we are. It is the Spirit who tells us we are sinners, in need of a Savior. It is the Spirit whose voice condemns us for the lies we tell, the angry words we spit out, the lustful desires we toy with. The Spirit draws us away from sin to the altar of repentance where Christ waits to forgive and to cleanse.

Through the renewing power of the Spirit we are made into a new creation. See this wonderful thing: a new man is created! Only God's Spirit can do that. We are born of the Spirit, born from above, renewed by the Holy Spirit.

But isn't Christ our Savior? Yes, but the Spirit is the active Agent through which faith in Christ gives us life in Christ. The New Testament calls Him "the Spirit of Christ." Remember, there is only one God. We know Christ because the Spirit brought us to Him, and Him to us. Christ died on the cross a long time ago. He is no longer here as men saw Him then. But the Spirit makes Him real to us today.

The Holy Spirit lives in us. We are His temple. When we put our trust in Christ, we open the doors for the Spirit to enter. Every true believer is the dwelling place of God through the Spirit. "He shall be in you," was the promise of Jesus. Paul says that Christ is in us. He is in us, even though He ascended to heaven. He is in us through His Spirit.

THE SPIRIT IS our Guide and Teacher. He is the Interpreter who instructs our minds in understanding the Bible. He tells us what we should do, and what we should not do. He is our Counselor in the choice of friends, of schools, of vocations, so that we can say with assurance, "The Lord told me." What would we do without a guide in the wilderness of this world?

The Holy Spirit is the power of God working in us. He not only teaches us; He gives us power to obey. It is through the Spirit that we overcome the sins of our nature. There are temptations and tendencies within us that tug us down. But there is also this Spirit within us who is a counteracting power, pulling us up.

The Holy Spirit changed Peter's self-confidence and pride to the humility he speaks of in his first epistle. The Holy Spirit changed John from the son of thunder of the Gospels to the apostle of love who speaks in his first epistle. The Holy Spirit cultivates within us that orchard whose fruit is "love, joy, peace, patience, kindness, goodness, faithfulness, self-control" (Galatians 5:22, 23).

William Temple once said, "It is no good giving me a play like *Hamlet* or *King Lear*, and telling me to write a play like that. Shakespeare could do it; I can't. And it is no good showing me a life like the life of Jesus and telling me to live a life like that. Jesus could do it; I can't. But if the genius of Shakespeare could come and live in me, then I could write plays like that. And if the Spirit of Jesus could come and live in me, then I could live a life like that."

The Spirit of Jesus does live within us, and if we let Him, He triumphs over every sin.

This power is ours for the taking. Think of it: God living in us!

For discussion:

1. How does the Bible explain the Trinity?
2. What are some of the Holy Spirit's tasks?
3. What is meant by the phrase "Christians are temples of the Holy Spirit"?
4. Describe the fruit of the Holy Spirit.

For your notebook:

Make a brief biblical study of the Holy Spirit. Use a concordance and list the times Holy Spirit (or a similar phrase) appears in each of the 66 books. Observe and summarize how God's Spirit worked in the time of the Bible. Write a one-page summary of your study.

8. WE BELONG TO THE CHURCH

We believe that the church is the body of Christ, the brotherhood of the redeemed, a disciplined people obedient to the Word of God, and a fellowship of love, intercession, and healing.

Did you ever see a Robinson Crusoe Christian? That's the kind that doesn't need the church. He's a Christian, he says, because he believes in Christ. But he thinks he can be a Christian by himself. He doesn't bother to join a church.

John Wesley once said there is no such thing as a solitary Christian. In the New Testament believers are always spoken of in a setting of other believers. There we see Christians living and worshiping and working in company with other Christians. These local companies are called churches. And Christ and His apostles said a great deal about the total group of Christians—the church.

Perhaps the Robinson Crusoe fellow doesn't understand what the church is. His confusion is understandable, for we mean a lot of different things when we talk about the "church."

Sometimes we mean a building, as when we describe a "beautiful church." And Crusoe doesn't care a bit about either the Washington Cathedral or a little cracker-box building out in the country. Sometimes we mean a particular service, as when we say we have Sunday school before "church."

Sometimes we mean a denomination, like the "Mennonite Church," and many a loner is scornful of all our divisions. Sometimes we mean the organized church—membership lists, constitutions, offices, program, hospitals and schools, and social service and missions. And it's all this that Crusoe wants to keep free from.

THIS CHURCH we belong to—what is it? It is made up of all those people who believe in Christ for their salvation. There has always been more than one of them. Each believer who is drawn to Christ and opens his heart to Him finds that others too have done the same. They have the same faith, the same Savior and Lord. They are filled with the same Holy Spirit. And so they share what they have in common; they belong to each other. This sharing company is the church.

If Robinson Crusoe would really believe in Christ, he would find these other believers, and joy in their fellowship. He is rejecting, not some fraternal or service club founded and conducted by men, but a fellowship planned and run by our Lord Himself.

36

WHAT GOOD does it do us to belong to the church? For one thing, there is much satisfaction in knowing that we are not alone in the world. Our loneliness is lost in the we-feeling of the people of God. No one of us is a people. But together we are "God's own people" (1 Peter 2:9).

At some one place there might be only a few of us. But worldwide we are a great company. The believers in Hokkaido and Java and Bihar and Tanzania and Rhodesia and Russia and Italy and Jamaica and Argentina and Brazil and Honduras and Mexico are our brothers and sisters. The redeemed in heaven will be a great multitude that no man can number, from every tribe and language, people and nation. It is good to love and be loved by someone of these now, and to know them personally.

In the church we learn from one another. Through teaching gifts from the Spirit and through age and experience, some of our fellow members are our teachers. We are all in a school together in which we learn what God's Word to us is, and how to apply it to life in North America in the latter third of the twentieth century. Together we learn better than we could learn alone.

Mountain climbers rope themselves together, so that if one slips, the others can keep him from sliding to injury or death. So in the church we are kept from moral dangers by the love, the warnings, the counsel, perhaps the discipline, of other members of the church.

As Christians we cannot follow the principles or the example of the sinful world about us. We must learn what God's will is, and obey it. Then we are disciples, followers of Christ. The church is a guide and stimulus in this.

THROUGH THE CHURCH we can serve. We might do something alone. But we would lack many of the opportunities the church gives us. In the church's program we can teach, sing, distribute literature, serve in hospitals, do relief work, participate in disaster service and servanthood work camps. The church trains us for this service in the local church program, in church schools, and in orientation centers. We are like an orchestra playing many instruments, but kept together by our Lord Conductor and His church.

Don't you find it lonesome and frustrating to toot out there all alone, Bob Crusoe? The Spirit and the church say, Come.

For discussion:

1. Discuss whether a person can be a Christian by himself.
2. What are some of the things people mean when they use the word "church"?
3. What good does it do to us to belong to the church?
4. What is your personal definition of "church"?

For your notebook:

Talk with three persons of varying backgrounds about their impressions of the church. Raise questions such as: What do you think the church is? Is the church keeping up with the times? In what ways do you think churches in our community make a difference in the life of the community? Write brief summaries of each conversation.

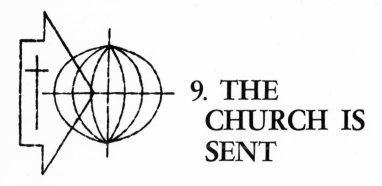

9. THE CHURCH IS SENT

We believe that Christ commissioned the church to go into all the world, making disciples of all the nations; and ministering to every human need.

God sent His Son into the world. Here He lived among men. He died and rose again for our salvation. In doing this He created the gospel, which means the good news.

News requires telling. This telling is the mission of the church. The One who sent His Son now sends the church. Jesus said to His disciples, "As my Father hath sent me, even so send I you." He said they should be His witnesses to the ends of the earth, and to the end of time. His last command was, "Go ye into all the world."

In August 1527 a number of Anabaptist leaders gathered in Augsburg, Germany, to look at their responsibil-

39

ity. Their rulers did not favor mission work. But these Christian leaders saw that only in being witnesses could they be a true church. And so with a map before them they divided the territory into which they would go two by two: Basel, Zurich, the Palatinate, Austria, Salzburg, Bavaria. They even discussed sending missionaries to the "red man beyond the sea."

Most of these "hedge preachers" soon were burned or drowned or beheaded. But they left us an example. Those who have heard the good news of the gospel cannot keep it to themselves. Knowing brings the responsibility of telling. The gospel is a stewardship, a trust, for which we must give an account.

GOD SENT His Son because He wants the world to be saved. God is not willing that any should perish. But no one can believe the gospel unless he hears. Those who know Christ must take part in His mission by helping others to know Him.

One of the reasons we band together in a church is that together we can spread the good news more effectively. As a church we can support missionaries where they could not go on their own. For three quarters of a century the Mennonite Church has had missionaries overseas, and so we have become an international church, a company that encircles the globe.

Our missionaries in more than a score of countries have been ambassadors for Christ. God in the beginning created of one blood all nations on earth, and now He is using the church to create a brotherhood in Christ of many nations and tongues.

But the church will fulfill its mission only as the individual members are witnesses. No one whom Christ has saved has a right to idleness or to selfish interests. Whatever may be his occupation, his real calling is to present Jesus Christ, and he must choose to work and live at the place where he can do this the best. "As you go, make disciples," said Jesus. Where you go and how you pay your fare is not as important as you bringing the gospel to someone.

The gospel is a story to be told, and that involves the use of words. But truly believing the gospel is behaving it as well as telling it. The world is full of need —sickness, ignorance, hunger, cold, loneliness, lack of opportunity for meaningful, satisfied living. Christian service to the destitute and the unfortunate, the victims of their own and others' sins, can preach the gospel too. People often do not understand what our words mean until we show them by our deeds.

Young Christians in our church today have a great opportunity to minister to human need. Work camps, Voluntary Service, Civilian Peace Service (in lieu of military service) bring us where the needy are. Here we can show love and compassion to the sick and the handicapped, to children and the aged. We can demonstrate what life is like when men live by love instead of by greed and hate.

IN SUCH SERVICE the Christ-spirit can be clearly seen. But there is need for the word too, to explain our motives and to point beyond ourselves to Christ. We need to keep word and deed close together, or our preaching overlooks real human needs, and our serving is merely human pity. We preach salvation through the cross of Christ, but the towel of service wins confidence and trust, and opens the way to choosing Christ.

Perhaps at Christmastime you sat at a long family table. If Uncle John, way down at the other end, said, "Please pass the bread," everybody stopped his own pressing business to supply Uncle's need. At the table of this world the supplies are not evenly distributed. War and famine fill the travel-ways with refugees. The ignorance and poverty of urban and rural ghettos close the doors to decent living. And an increasing proportion of the world's people do not know Christ, the Living Bread.

This complex of need gives the church its mission. And me. And you.

For discussion:

1. What is the church for?
2. What is the calling of each Christian?
3. What is the gospel?
4. How is the gospel best shared? How are words and deeds related?

For your notebook:

Write to a volunteer in a service or mission assignment, preferably one with whom you are personally acquainted. Ask that he share with you his understanding of what it means for the church to be in mission, to share the good news. Keep a copy of your letter and the reply for your notebook.

10. THE CHURCH NEEDS MINISTERS

We believe it is the will of God that there should be ministers to teach the Word, to serve as leaders, to administer the ordinances, to lead the church in the exercise of discipline, and to serve as pastors and teachers.

The former minister of the church has died, or retired, or moved to another church, or to another type of service. The church needs someone to take his place.

A new minister has been selected. He may have been brought in from another church. Or he may have just graduated from the seminary, and has been recommended by the Ministerial Committee of the conference.

Or the congregation may have decided to call one of its own lay members to become their minister. They may vote on who this person should be. If most of the votes were for Jonathan Martin, he is today being ordained to the ministry. If the votes were scattered, some of our churches will use the lot. The approved candidates sit on the front bench of the church, waiting to see which one the Lord has chosen. After the sermon, small books, all alike and as many as there are candidates, are placed on the table before them. In one of these books a slip of paper—the lot—has been placed inside the front cover. Each man takes a book. These are opened by the officiating bishop, and the man in whose book the slip is found is considered the Lord's choice.

However he is chosen, he now kneels as a symbol of his becoming a servant of the congregation. One or more church officials, as representatives of the church, lay their hands on his head. He is told what his responsibilities shall be, and there is a prayer of consecration, asking God's blessing on this new servant of the church.

If the new minister has been ordained earlier, at some other church, he will not be ordained, but installed in his new responsibility. Whatever the process, the church calls the minister; he does not call himself.

Why does the church call a man to be a minister?

It is not to set him apart in a special holy order. The minister should be a good example, but all the church members are expected to live a holy life.

It is not to set him above the rest of the church in a place of honor, so that he can be called "reverend" and get discounts and other special privileges. The minister is just one of the brotherhood; the word "minister" means servant. The Bible says he is not to lord it over the other members. He should be respected, but not put on a pedestal. Our pulpits are higher than the floor level only so that the speaker can be seen.

Ordaining a man does not mean that the church members expect him to do the work of the church. All members carry responsibilities and should do whatever their gifts fit them for. The Christian ministry is not just a profession, the way some men make their living. The church should support the minister so that he has time for his duties. But no one should become a minister for the sake of the money he will get.

The church calls an ordained man to special tasks. One of them is preaching. A minister is often called a preacher because he is expected to preach: to explain the Bible and to call people to faith in Christ and to holy living.

Ministers are expected to baptize new Christians, to serve communion, to perform marriage ceremonies, to anoint the sick, to organize the church into a working team, to teach the members how to witness in the community, to lead the church in keeping standards of Christian conduct.

The minister is available to talk over with people any problems they may have. In this way he helps them to grow in the spiritual life.

The minister is the worship leader of the congregation. He plans the worship service, and helps the people to realize that God is with them as they sing, pray, bring their offerings, listen to the preaching, and instruct one another.

The minister helps the church to recognize the needs for Christian service in the community and in the world. He encourages the members to go where the needs are, and to use their means and their talents in a feeding, healing, comforting ministry.

The minister is one of the representatives of the congregation in the sessions of the area conference. The congregation makes him available for denominational and community assignments in boards, committees, and evangelistic outreach.

I thought from early boyhood that I would become a

preacher. Many ministers knew they had a call from God before the church said anything about it. A minister ought to know that God has called him. But this inner call must be tested by the judgment of the church. If the church doesn't call us, we find other ways to serve.

Years ago young men being baptized were asked to promise to be willing to preach if the church should call them. This was good. During the teen years, when many people decide on their lifework, Christian young men ought to consider whether God wants them in the ministry.

It is a good thing to talk to one's pastor about any call one may feel to preach the gospel. And if one has a call, he ought to prepare himself for this future service as minister of the gospel.

For discussion:

1. What would happen in your congregation if your present pastor were suddenly called away?

2. What is the purpose of ordination?

3. What are some of the jobs a minister needs to do?

4. What initiative dare a young man take if he has interests in becoming a minister?

For your notebook:

Write a brief report of what your minister does as you understand it. Then discuss your report with him and rewrite it, taking into account the ideas he provides. Notice the differences between your perception of what he does and what he reports that he actually does. In your final report suggest ways that he might do a better job as a pastor. Be constructive and helpful in your criticism.

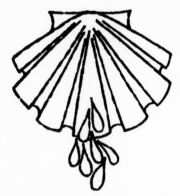

11. WE RECEIVE BAPTISM

We believe that those who repent and believe should be baptized with water as a symbol of baptism with the Spirit, cleansing from sin, and commitment to Christ.

In Switzerland, in 1525, a group of Christian believers were meeting in a home. Hans Bruggbach confessed his sins and asked to be baptized as a sign of his conversion. Felix Manz took a kitchen dipper and poured water upon his head, "in the name of God the Father, God the Son, and God the Holy Spirit."

So thousands of others, all of whom had been baptized as babies, asked to be rebaptized. They had come to believe that infant baptism, as observed in all the state churches of the time, was not a true Christian baptism.

They came to be called Anabaptists, which means rebaptizers. The new baptism was against the law, and many of the Anabaptists, or Brethren, as they called themselves, were imprisoned, tortured, and killed by burning or drowning.

What is it they were willing to do at the risk of death? Certainly men would not die simply for the privilege of having water poured on them! These Anabaptists, who are the spiritual fathers of the Mennonites, got some new understandings of what baptism means. To be faithful to the New Testament they wanted believer's baptism.

TODAY WE DON'T talk about baptism. We seldom ask, "Have you been baptized?" We would rather ask, "Are you a Christian?" or "What does Christ mean to you?"

But still we are baptized. Perhaps we take it for granted. Do we know, as our persecuted fathers did, what baptism really means?

Water baptism does not make us Christians. In the Middle Ages conquered peoples were baptized forcibly as they were driven through rivers. That kind of baptism did nothing for them but make them wet. Baptizing a baby may do nothing for him but make him cry. H_2O can't wash away our sins.

Jesus commanded the apostles to preach the gospel, and when people believe, to baptize them. The New Testament says more about baptism than any other sacrament or ordinance. It is clearly the will of God that believers in Christ should be baptized.

And yet just blind obedience is a poor reason for being baptized. If we don't understand what is happening, probably nothing important *is* happening. To be effective our baptism must be intelligent. Youth of the age for which these studies are written are just at the age when most of them are baptized. What is this action a symbol or sign of?

BAPTISM IS a sign of an inner cleansing. Water is used to wash with, and is a good symbol for God's way of taking away the filth of our sin. Water baptism does not cause this cleansing; it only testifies that the waters of inner baptism have done their work.

Baptism is a sign of a new life in the Spirit. The Holy Spirit is poured out on those who believe in Christ. The Bible says that by one Spirit we are all baptized into one body. Only those belong to Christ who have His Spirit. Water baptism is an outward and public testimony of the inner baptism of the Spirit. Baptism does not bring the Spirit; it testifies that He has come.

Baptism is a sign of a life commitment to Christ. It is a way of making a pledge or promise. When we are baptized, the minister asks, "Do you promise to submit yourself to Christ and His Word, and faithfully to abide in the same until death?" And we answer, "I do." The minister hears that promise, the congregation hears it, and God hears it. We have committed ourselves. We must understand what we are promising, and we must make this promise of our own free will.

Baptism is a sign that we are leaving sin. We promise "to renounce Satan, the world, and all the works of darkness," and our own "sinful desires." To the Anabaptist it was a pledge to be faithful even unto death. And it's the same for us—until death, if not to the death of martyrdom. Jesus speaks of a baptism of suffering, and we must be ready for this. In baptism we publicly enlist ourselves as disciples, following Christ wherever He may lead us. We should be baptized only when we are ready.

And baptism is a symbol of our acceptance by the church. In granting us baptism the congregation says it wants us as members. We have their assurance that they have seen in us the qualifications of membership. And we accept the obligations of church membership: to carry the responsibilities of service, to share our gifts and possessions with the other members, to participate in the

49

fellowship of discipline. In baptism we promise this to our fellow believers.

THIS MAKES IT clear why baptism is not for babies. Children cannot hear the Word, cannot feel conviction for sin, cannot promise to forsake sin and live a life of discipleship. Baptism is for those who want it, who have turned to the Lord in penitence and faith, who intend, by God's grace, to "walk in newness of life."

The meaning of baptism is more important than the mode. The New Testament does not tell us how to baptize. Churches through the centuries have either put the applicant into the water (immersion) or put the water on the applicant (affusion). Each mode has some good symbolism in it. Most Mennonites have followed most of the Anabaptists in using pouring. It is a practical form of baptism: a dying man can't be immersed.

But the way it is done is not too important. Most important is that what happens on the inside and outside are united in one true baptism.

For discussion:

1. Why did the Anabaptists insist on rebaptism?

2. Explain three ways in which baptism is a sign.

3. Why do you think babies should not be baptized?

4. Of what significance is the mode or the way in which we are baptized?

For your notebook:

Prepare a one-page report of the way in which the Anabaptists were persecuted because of their beliefs about baptism in the early 1500's. Use the *Martyrs Mirror* and the article on "Martyrs" in the *Mennonite Encyclopedia* as resources.

12. WE REMEMBER CHRIST'S DEATH

We believe that the church should observe the communion of the Lord's Supper as a symbol of His broken body and shed blood, and of the fellowship of His church, until His return.

We act out our faith! The use of drama to express an idea is usually effective. For drama uses two symbols: the symbol of word and the symbol of action. And the action helps to show what the word means.

The most common symbolic act of the Christian faith is the communion, sometimes called the Lord's Supper. We are baptized only once, but we partake of the emblems of bread and wine again and again.

Jesus instituted this ordinance and He commanded His followers to use this sign to remind them of how He died for their sins.

In the drama of the communion we use eating and drinking, two very common human actions. They help us to remember the central Christian truth, that Christ saved us by dying on the cross.

The bread, broken from the larger pieces, represents the body of Christ, broken by the sin of the world. The wine, which is usually called the "cup," is in its color a vivid representation of the blood which Jesus shed.

As we eat this bread and drink this grape juice, we act out our taking Jesus by faith as our Savior. Every time we take communion we show that Jesus did something that can save us, and that by faith we accept what He did.

WE DO NOT BELIEVE that merely taking the communion gives us spiritual life, any more than being baptized washes away our sins. But our realization of salvation becomes stronger and clearer as we act out the truth we have received about how our very life comes from Him.

We don't each one go off to ourselves to observe this memorial service. We act it out together as a congregation of believers. This is a symbol too. It shows that we share a common faith. The loaf from which the bit of bread is broken is a unit made from many grains of wheat. The juice in the cup is made from many grapes. So we observe the communion, not as individuals, but as the people of God, the church, united in faith and in mutual concern.

This means that only true believers may participate. I must examine myself, not to see whether I am good enough to partake, but to see whether I really believe in what we are acting out. The church is responsible to invite to the Lord's table only those who are truly His. For if we eat and drink together, we must be willing to live together in a common obedience.

And there must be no cliques, no separation among u'

because of wealth or education or race. It does not make any difference whom you sit beside on communion Sunday. The ground is level before the cross.

It is only important that we be prepared in mind and heart. In many of our churches we make special effort in a counsel meeting to see that all are at peace with God and with each other. We cannot receive the symbol of the Lord's grace if we do not have gracious forgiveness of one another.

SO WE COME to the communion. We are about to go through again the most important event that ever happened in history. The drama of the Lord's Supper will help us to bring it vividly to mind.

"Were you there when they crucified my Lord?"

No, you weren't. But now in memory, according to the record you have read and the retelling of it in the sermon, you are carried back to that time. You survey the cross "on which the Prince of glory died." You see and hear as sin's enmity breaks the body of the Son of God. You understand how God poured out life to absorb the hate of men. And you know once again that Christ is hanging on that cross for you, and that by His death you live.

And so, as the minister holds the symbols in his hands and thanks God for the broken body and the shed blood of Christ, your own heart overflows with gratefulness. And you purpose in your heart that you will live for Him who died for you.

THE DETAILS of the observance are not important, so long as we hold the vital meaning of what we are doing. Whether a bishop or a minister is in charge; whether the bread is leavened or unleavened; whether you drink from one cup or from individual cups; whether the emblems are carried to you, or you go forward to receive them; whether communion is held once a week or once a year, on regular or special occasions: these things we can fit into according to the customs of the congregation.

Are we happy in the communion service, or very sober, even sad? There is sadness, of course, in remembering how Jesus had to die for us. And we ought to be reverent, almost in awe, before the tremendous importance of our dramatic action. But salvation brings joy. We partake of the communion, not with lightness, but with a deep rejoicing in what God has done for us. In the communion we do look back to Christ's suffering. But we also look forward to the glorious victory of Christ's coming again, when we shall eat with Him in His kingdom.

For discussion:

1. Of what value is the repetition of the communion service?

2. What is the meaning of the bread in the service?

3. What is the meaning of the juice in the service?

4. Why is communion conducted with other people rather than alone?

For your notebook:

Interview three older persons—a Mennonite, another Protestant, and a Roman Catholic. Ask them to explain what the ordinance (or a sacrament as they may know it) of the Lord's Supper means and also to describe for you one of the most meaningful communions in which they have participated. Write a summary comparing and contrasting the responses which you get.

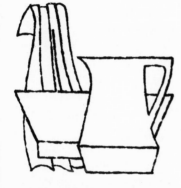

13. WE LOVE AND SERVE

We believe in the washing of the saints' feet as a symbol of brotherhood, cleansing, and service, and in giving the right hand of fellowship and the holy kiss as symbols of Christian love.

"My brother, I love you!" This every Christian says to every other Christian. A Christian who hates is a Christian only in name. Love is the central Christian virtue. God is love, and because we are the children of God, it is our nature to love. "Little children, love one another." And big children too.

There are many ways to say, "I love you." There are times to say it in words. And there are times when actions speak louder than words. We show that we love through a friendly smile and greeting, or through hospitable entertainment, or through helpful assistance and the sharing of our goods to meet emergency needs.

FROM THE BIBLE we get two symbolic actions which show Christian love. One is the holy kiss. Five times in the epistles we are told to greet one another with a holy kiss. This symbol of love and fellowship has been used through the centuries as a sign and seal of brotherhood in the church. Our Anabaptist fathers used it; we are told in *Martyrs Mirror* that men would kiss each other before they went to the stake or bowed before the swordsman.

Where men and women call each other brother and sister, as we do in the Mennonite Church, the holy kiss fits into the family atmosphere. Its use shows a genuine and sincere affection for those who are close to one another because they are one in Christ.

The kiss has a twofold use. One is in salutation, whenever two brethren or two sisters meet, and show their fellowship in this greeting. This is less common than it used to be. The other use is in connection with rituals or ceremonies. We were all received into church with a kiss, which showed acceptance. When two persons participate in a foot-washing service, they follow the mutual washing with a kiss of peace, as the Anabaptists called it. In an ordination service the ordained man and the one who ordains him kiss one another. And in some marriage ceremonies the new husband and wife kiss each other, a formal symbol of their new relationship.

The holy kiss is always in combination with the right hand of fellowship. Sometimes the hand of fellowship only is in good taste, as between the sexes (except husband and wife) and in situations where the kiss would be misinterpreted. In Latin America the embrace is a suitable substitute.

THE SECOND FORMAL symbol of Christian love

which we use is foot-washing. This is based on the story in John 13 of how Jesus, on the night before His crucifixion, washed the feet of His disciples. Although He was their Lord and Master, He acted the part of a servant, which apparently none of His disciples were willing to do. They had been arguing about places of honor, and He gave them an unforgettable demonstration of humility and loving service.

In this He was an example that we should follow. When He came to earth, He came as a servant. He came to minister unto others. This foot-washing episode was a supreme example of His servanthood role. The vivid detail of the story shows the deep impression it made on John. Jesus here gave an acted parable of how love makes one serve. And He commanded His disciples to wash one another's feet as He had washed theirs. "For I have given you an example, that you also should do as I have done to you" (John 13:15).

How can we follow the example of Jesus? Most of all, by doing deeds of service with a heart of love. Important is the constant attitude which impels us, any day and every day, to be of service in the church, and to all who need it.

We become servants in work camps, Voluntary Service, Pax, Mennonite Disaster Service, WMSA and GMSA, service aspects of our mission program—these are ways of washing feet. When the love put in our hearts by the Holy Spirit drives us out into service to anyone, anytime, anywhere—then we are washing feet.

But it helps also to have a church ordinance which dramatizes the spirit of servanthood. This we have in the foot-washing service observed twice a year in most of our churches. Usually we pair up, men with men and women with women, for the sake of modesty. Each in turn kneels before the other and moistens both his feet in a tub, and then dries them with a towel. By this act we pledge ourselves to be loving servants of one another. The meaning of the symbol is still very plain today.

In answering Peter's objections Jesus made foot-washing a symbol also of cleansing. They had already been bathed, He says, which is the basic cleansing of the heart. Now they only need, He suggests, the lesser washing of the feet, to wash away the soiling of the day's walk. So foot-washing shows that Christ cleanses us and keeps us clean. We "remember by this foot-washing the true washing" is the way the Dordrecht Confession points out the spiritual sense that underlies the symbol.

Various branches of Mennonites, Brethren, and Baptists use this ceremony. The Roman Catholic pope on each Maundy Thursday washes the feet of twelve selected persons. In the Middle Ages it was often made a pompous ceremony, observed at coronations and installations. Waldenses and Albigenses made it again a religious rite. Many Anabaptists, but not all, adopted it, yet used it sometimes only to welcome guests into the home. The Dordrecht Confession of 1632 included foot-washing as a Christian symbol. Our branch of the church practices it, but in the Franconia Conference only since 1900.

When practiced in a proper spirit, and with good decorum, these symbols add to the meaning of the Christian faith. Those are happy who do them!

For discussion:

1. What are appropriate times for using the holy kiss today?

2. Where does the idea of foot-washing come from?

3. What is the meaning of the foot-washing service?
4. Is foot-washing only a Mennonite practice?

For your notebook:

Read John 13 in at least three different translations and then try to write a translation or paraphrase of your own. Be as imaginative as you can in translating the event from century one into century twenty.

14. FAITH AFFECTS RELATION- SHIPS

We believe that God has established unique roles for man and woman, symbolized by man's bared head in praying and prophesying, and by woman's veiled head.

In sections 11-14 of the *Mennonite Confession of Faith* (1963) we look at several outward signs and symbols of truths in which we believe. Water baptism and the communion service represent primarily our vertical relationship to God. Foot-washing represents primarily a horizontal relationship of service to our fellowmen.

There is another symbol which speaks of a horizontal relationship, that between man and woman. When men worship or pray in any church service, their heads should be uncovered. When women worship or pray or teach in the church, their heads should be covered.

Most Christian people show some awareness of this symbol. A man would not think of sitting in church with his hat on. And women of most churches would feel it improper to go to a church service bareheaded.

But what is the meaning of this symbol—the uncovered head for man and the covered head for woman? Many people observe the sign without knowing what is being signified. It is important, not only to do the right things, but to do them intelligently, for the right reasons. Christian practices must be filled with Christian meanings.

The Bible teaching on this subject is found in Paul's first letter to the Corinthians, chapter 11. What is taught there agrees with other Bible teaching on the relationship of man and woman. Paul tells us here that God has written it into the nature of things that man is the head of woman, and that woman should recognize that headship. As Christ acknowledges the headship of the Father, and as man acknowledges subjection to Christ, so the woman acknowledges the headship of man.

This does not mean that woman is inferior to man. Christianity, as compared with other religions, gives a high place to woman. She has her gifts, and a right and privilege to use them. But there are functions that belong to man, and not to woman. A woman is gifted and called primarily to teach and to serve. Man is gifted and called to manage and administer. Man and woman are equal in their need of God's grace. And alike they share in God's forgiveness and in the gifts of the Spirit.

Of all this the covering is a sign. When a woman veils herself in worship, she is accepting man's leadership in the church. She is saying, to herself and to others, that she wants to take her place in the work of the church. She is stepping into her place of privilege, working with man in the order that God has established. Her covering keeps reminding her of that order. It urges her to remember that she is a helper, not the manager.

She finds joy in knowing that she willingly fits into the arrangement that God made when He created the human race, male and female. She does not want to be involved in a battle of the sexes. She wants to avoid the unhappiness of a woman who insists on having her own way.

THE WEDDING VEIL which many brides use is a remnant of an older costume that symbolized the subjection of a wife to her husband. Whether she realizes it or not, the bridal veil says the bride is coming under the leadership of the bridegroom. Just so all the women of the church wear the head-covering to show their relationship to all the men of the church.

Paul says it was the practice of all the churches that the woman should be veiled during prayer and testimony. Tertullian, a churchman of the second century, says that all women wore veils in the churches established by the apostles. This is a Christian practice of long standing.

The Corinthian passage also tells us that the veiling matches the longer hair of the woman, and the bare head of the man matches his shorter hair.

The form of the veiling the Bible does not specify. Probably the veiling of the Corinthian women was a garment which all women of the time wore. Into the wearing of this garment Paul put a spiritual meaning for its use in the church. On mission fields the form of the covering can be determined by what is possible in the various cultures.

The white net covering now worn by women of our Mennonite Church in America has developed from a head-covering once worn by women of central Europe. It serves very well now as a covering worn especially to symbolize the place of women in the church. It is easily carried, and it goes well with any modest dress. It fits the requirement of simplicity. It is not the only possible form, but it is serving the purpose well. If we did not have this pattern, we should have to agree on something else. The symbol is more meaningful if it is accepted by many. Something worn on the head outdoors is often not thought of as a symbol at all.

As with all symbols, the outward form is not nearly so important as the truth or the attitude symbolized. In fact, a covering on the head of a bold, boisterous, bossy woman, because it would be inconsistent, would mean nothing. Wearing a covering does not make one a Christian, nor does it itself produce the attitude it symbolizes.

But as a response and symbol of what God has done in the heart of a Christian girl or woman, it is a beautiful and effective sign.

For discussion:

1. Review the outward signs which Mennonites practice and explain their meaning.

2. What is the biblical basis for women having their heads covered in worship?

3. What does the head-covering symbolize?

4. Of what value is this symbol?

For your notebook:

Check two commentaries (such as Erdman's, Barclay's, or the Layman's Bible Commentary) on 1 Corinthians 11 and summarize the two views on the head-covering which you find in the commentary. Compare the views briefly with your own understanding on the basis of this section.

15. MARRIAGE SHOULD BE CHRISTIAN

We believe that Christian marriage is intended by God to be the union of one man and one woman for life, and that Christians shall marry only in the Lord.

Not everyone can or should observe all the ordinances of the church. Some of them are only for some people.

Only believers should be baptized. Neither baptism nor any other ordinance has meaning for little children. And baptism is normally experienced only once by any one person.

All Christians should from time to time participate in the communion service and in foot-washing.

The kiss of love is for all, on appropriate occasions, but only men with men, and women with women.

The anointing with oil as a symbol of the Lord's healing is for the sick, and many of us may never call for this.

The veiling of the head in worship is only for women.

Ordination, symbolized by the laying of hands upon the head, is only for certain ones whom the Lord calls to special responsibilities as church leaders.

Likewise marriage may not be for everybody. Jesus and Paul were not married. Many good people have found it better for one reason or other to live unmarried. It is wiser to remain single than to enter into a marriage that is outside the will of God for us.

For most of us marriage is within the will of God. God created us male and female, and intended that a man and a woman should marry, live together, and have children. Sex is one of God's good gifts to us, and it finds its natural and holy use in marriage.

A CHRISTIAN MARRIAGE, however, is much more than sexual. A husband and wife are married in heart and mind as well as in body. It is life's closest relationship, and brings a lifetime of love and joy if the marriage is truly Christian.

Young people in our culture may choose their life partners. But the process of choosing needs careful control. Successful marriages are produced by wise choices and by a courtship that looks for mental and spiritual fitness as well as good looks. Fornication is a sin, even in these days when so many people argue that it isn't. And it is likely to hurry teenagers into an early marriage that may not be a happy one.

Choosing a life partner is one of life's most important decisions. Most people need some counsel on this: from parents, from pastors, from youth counselors in school or church, and from the reading of good books. Here are some principles that may help one in his choice:

1. Adjustments in marriage are easier when husband

and wife come from a similar background.

2. Choose someone that you know well. It is good to know the family too. Most people reflect the homes from which they come.

3. Christians should marry "only in the Lord." The closest relationship calls for unity in basic matters.

4. Religious agreement is important. Interchurch marriages have problems, and make problems for the children.

5. You are choosing for life—"for as long as you both shall live." It is a sin to put away one partner and marry another.

Marriages create homes. Babies are born into families and are trained and brought to maturity there. But as these new adults choose partners, they set up new homes. God said that a person should forsake his father and mother and stick to his married partner. Gradually through his teens he has grown in independence. Now in marriage he has found a new loyalty. Parents may still be available for advice when he wants them. And he has certain obligations to his parents as long as they live. But his chief responsiblities are toward his own new home. No one is ready for marriage until he is willing and able to carry those responsibilities.

TEENAGERS should be learning what makes a home happy. They read directions from the Bible. They see the importance of love and helpfulness and faithfulness. They learn the effectiveness of the kind word and the meek spirit. They become accustomed to obedience and respect. It becomes clear to them that the three-car family, with a big modern house and a private swimming pool, is not necessarily the happy family. They experience, or perhaps can only observe, that the family which puts God first, which reads and obeys the Bible, which attends and works in the church, is the happy family.

Marriage is an ordinance of the church, and so should have a religious ceremony, with members of the church as witnesses. A license to marry must be secured from the state, but the pastor or some other church official should say the solemn words which declare that two have become one. It should be a sacred and joyous occasion, with the plans worked out in full cooperation with the officiating minister. It should not be a style show, directed by the etiquette book. It should not be interrupted or marred by picture-taking or jokesters.

It should be the desire of every young Christian to find and to do the Lord's will in his courtship, in the marriage ceremony, and in the setting up of his new home. Failure here is truly tragic, and success here is truly blessed.

For discussion:

1. How can successful marriage be insured?
2. What things should a person contemplating marriage consider?
3. What should teenagers be learning about marriage in their parental homes?
4. Why is marriage an ordinance of the church?

For your notebook:

Write a brief essay on "Qualities I Would Like in My Mate." Explain particularly what place you feel Christian faith should have as you approach marriage. You should find helpful resources in your school or church library for this report.

16. WE FOLLOW CHRIST

We believe that Christians are not to be conformed to the world, but should seek to conform to Christ in every area of life.

Years ago I read a satire called "The Christian Bite." It told of a lion which had developed an appetite for the persecuted Christians who were thrown into his den. He no longer liked any other kind of meat. This lion was sold to another city, and his new keepers were told that he must be fed only Christians.

But the Christian church in this second city had fallen away from the standards of life which set Christians off from the rest of society. They had come to talk and act and look just like everybody else. They drank and caroused like the other citizens. They lived in the same luxury and impurity. They went to the same amusements; they laughed at the same jokes. And the poor lion had to go hungry because in this city they couldn't tell which were the Christians!

The satire is effective because we all know that if you couldn't tell they were Christians, they weren't.

WE BELIEVE THAT Christians are different from non-Christians. Because they have a Christian faith, they live a Christian life. The two must go together.

The Bible is very clear in showing the contrast between the Christian church of born-again believers and the unbelieving world of sinning men and women. Paul says we shall not be conformed to the world, which means that we shall not be pressed into its mold. Believers shall not be mismated with unbelievers, for what has a believer in common with an unbeliever? What fellowship can light have with darkness? Because we belong to God, we do not belong to the world. Because we follow Christ, we do not follow Satan.

As believers in Christ, we become His disciples. A disciple is a learner, a follower. We are committed to do God's will, and we honestly try to find out what that will is. And when we know what He wants us to do, then by the strength He gives, we do it.

This is not easy. It is hard to be a real Christian because we are born with a nature which in many ways is contrary to God's will. The Bible draws an ugly picture of the works of our sinful flesh: immorality, strife, jealousy, anger, selfishness, envy, carousing. It is easy to slip into these sins, even when we are trying to be Christians.

Moreover, the world about us tries to pull us away from Christ. We have a strong tendency to be like those around us. It is easy to get our standards of right and

69

wrong from what other people do. More than 50 percent of one group of Mennonite young people admitted that they decide on what is right or wrong by what most people do.

If most people use profanity, they think it can't be very wrong. If the rest of the class cheats in schoolwork, they go along with the crowd. If others go to dances, they feel they may too. If cigarettes are "in," then they don't want to be "out."

OF COURSE a thing is not wrong just because everybody does it. It is not wrong to drive on the right side of the road. It is not wrong to eat with a fork. It is not wrong for a man to wear trousers or for a girl to wear a dress. It is not wrong to go to school. We have no call as Christians to challenge our culture at every point. We don't need to be different just to be different.

But we live in a sinful, sick world, that walks in darkness and disobedience. Many things that most people do are against the holiness which God commands. Time and again the Christian must say "No" to the pressures of the world, because his life is ordered by the Word of God.

When we become Christians, we turn from sin, and turn to the Lord. We no longer love the world and its ways. Now we live "in Christ." We put off the things that belong to Satan and his crowd. We put on the ways of Christ and His people. The Spirit which dwells within us makes us different. Salvation is not genuine unless it makes us live a Christian life. Loyalty to Christ means that we do not dally with anything that we know is wrong. "What would Christ have me to do?" has more influence than "What do others do?"

There is danger that we accept some few symbols of separation from the world, and yet remain carnal and worldly in heart. Obedience to Christ affects every area of life.

It calls us to truthfulness and cleanness and kindness of speech. It calls us to leave out recreation or amusement, like gambling, which has something unchristian in it. It makes us remember that our bodies are holy temples, not to be defiled with tobacco, drugs, liquor, or sexual sins.

Christian obedience leads us to the ornament of a beautiful spirit, instead of jewelry and fine clothes and cosmetics. It makes us keep money and possessions in a lower place. It will not let us show off in any way, by immodest clothing, by display of fine cars and expensive homes and furnishings.

Obedience to Christ gives us love for all men, even those who mistreat us. It keeps us from hatred and malice, from war and violence of any kind. It gives us respect for sacred things: the Bible, which is the Word of God; the church, which is the people of God; the Lord's day, set apart for worship and Christian service. It makes friendship unselfish, and courtship pure and unstained.

Our separation will not keep us away from people—just from their sins. We are to shine as lights, out where the darkness is. We are healing agents in a sick world; good neighbors in a hungry, lonely world; witnesses of the truth in a lost world. And the way we live shows the meaning of what we say.

For discussion:

1. Why are Christians different from non-Christians?

2. Why is it hard to be a Christian?
3. What is involved in "turning from sin"?
4. What is involved in obeying Christ?

For your notebook:

Nonconformity is an idea which is sometimes difficult to get hold of. Writing a short report may help you to focus some thoughts on the topic. Begin by asking three people in your congregation what nonconformity means. Check those findings against the dictionary definition and other printed resources such as the article on "Nonconformity" in the *Mennonite Encyclopedia* and *Separated unto God* by J. C. Wenger.

17. WE TELL THE TRUTH

We believe that Christians are to be open and transparent in life, ever speaking the truth, and employing no oaths.

A witness appears in court, to be questioned and to tell what he knows about the case up for trial. Before he says anything, he is put under oath, swearing with upraised hand that he will tell the truth.

But he may be a Christian who has read the command of Jesus, "Do not swear at all." And so he may ask the official to substitute for the usual oath a simple affirmation. American and Canadian courts have held that this is permissible, and they allow this substitution in any court or on any legal papers. We are fortunate to live in countries which guarantee religious freedom. Exemption from the legal oath is one aspect of this freedom.

In the Old Testament all oaths were to be by the name of God, and not by some false god. In the New

Testament, however, there is more emphasis on the inner truthfulness which makes the oath unnecessary, and so all swearing is forbidden. James says that our yes is to be simply yes, and our no is to be a simple no.

EARLY CHRISTIANS went by this rule until the coming of the state church. The oath was fully accepted by the Catholic and Reformed churches. But the Anabaptists, seeking to restore New Testament standards, refused to swear. The first Anabaptist confession said that the gospel "forbids Christians all swearing." All the later confessions repeat this rule. More than any other Anabaptist principle, all branches of Mennonites in all countries have stood for this biblical command.

The refusal to take an oath is grounded on a deep and solid foundation. For truth and honesty of heart is a basic Christian characteristic. We tell the truth because it is right to do so. We know that the Lord hates a lying tongue, and that all liars have their destiny in the lake of fire. God has written truth in our hearts. The Spirit that dwells in us is a Spirit of truth, and not of lying.

The oath is used to make people afraid to lie. It is required because ordinary statements are so often false. In the oath the swearer calls God to witness to what he is saying. He at least implies that he wants a curse to come upon him if he has not spoken the truth. And legally he is guilty of perjury if what he says under oath is false.

Actually, the oath does not compel truth-telling. Two people, both under oath to tell the truth and nothing but the truth, will contradict each other. An honest man without an oath is more dependable than a dishonest man under oath. The essayist Charles Lamb once said that the oath is unnecessary for Quakers because they tell the truth without it. That should be true of Mennonites too.

In fact, the use of an oath may dull our sense of truth by its implication that we must tell the truth only when sworn to do so. Rejecting the oath binds one always to be truthful, always to be so open and transparent of life that people will believe his simple affirmations. The one who refuses to swear is saying that for him absolute truth is a part of following Jesus. He may be at times mistaken, and so unintentionally untrue. But he never tries to deceive.

THERE ARE KINDS of swearing other than the legal oath. The oath may be profanity, using holy names lightly, as in "by God" and "by heaven." Some people may be ignorant of the meaning of some of their expressions: "by George" is an oath by St. George of England. We may count on it that any "by" words are historic oaths.

Some people do not dare to use real oaths because they sound like swearing. However, they do use, often ignorantly, "minced oaths," shortened and round-about forms which have oath origins. "My goodness" means "my God." "Gee" is the first syllable of "Jesus." "Golly" is a euphemism for "God." "Heck" is a substitute for "hell." The biblical rule is a safe one: let your yes be yes, and your no be no.

The use of the oath is one of the things that keeps us from becoming a part of certain organizations, like fraternities, and sororities, and lodges. Masons swear never to divulge the secrets of the lodge, and ask that if they should ever do so, their tongues may be torn out by the roots.

THE SECRECY of the secret orders, or lodges, violates the transparency which the Christian should strive for. Jesus said, "In secret have I done nothing." The lodges may do some good things. But there are many features about them that are unchristian, in addition to their oaths. They use titles, such as "Worshipful Master," in a way that violates true brotherhood.

They demand a loyalty between the members that goes above loyalty to the church. They promise a way of salvation other than through Christ, whose name is excluded from their ritual. The lodge really sets up a religion, with its requirements, its belief in a Supreme Being, its fraternal relations, and its ritual of worship, that is a substitute for Christianity.

We believe in a truthfulness and openness of heart that needs no oaths, and has no place for secrecy.

For discussion:

1. What is the difference between an oath and an affirmation?
2. Why did the Anabaptists refuse to swear?
3. What is the purpose of the oath?
4. What is a minced oath?

For your notebook:

Prepare a short paper on a secret society such as the Masons or Elks. Dig out some basic information from a reputable general encyclopedia. Check those facts with a member of the organization you are writing about in your own community. Be as specific as possible in your research.

18. GOD LOVES THROUGH US

We believe that it is the will of God for Christians to refrain from force and violence in human relations and to show Christian love to all men.

The enemies of Jesus had hounded Him for months. In Galilee or Judea, they were there to contradict Him and to plot against Him. In synagogues and marketplaces, on streets and in houses, in the temple area and in the trial hall at Jerusalem, they had lied about Him and spit out their venomous hatred.

Now they had Him where they wanted Him—on a Roman cross. Their maneuvering had been successful, and they cackled their exaltation. "Let the . . . King of Israel come down now from the cross," they mocked.

How did Jesus react to all this? "When he was abused he did not retort with abuse, when he suffered he uttered no threats" (1 Peter 2:23, NEB). He offered no resistance, although He could have called legions of angels to His defense. He said that if His kingdom were of this world, His followers would be fighting to save Him from arrest. But He restrained them when they wanted to, telling them that from sword-taking comes perishing. As the nails were biting into His hands, He prayed, "Father, forgive them."

He was acting out His own teaching: offering the other cheek to the one who slaps you, giving your coat to the man who takes your shirt, walking two miles with the man who forces you to walk one, loving your enemies. These are His commands. It is the way He would have His followers live.

Other New Testament commandments fit these. Paul asks us to live at peace with all men, not to seek revenge, to feed the hungry enemy, to use good to defeat evil. To Christians suing each other in the law courts he asks, Why not rather let yourselves be robbed?

Peter tells us to take Christ as an example of nonresistant suffering. Christ is called the Prince of Peace, and His disciples are to have a temper of mind like His.

GOD IS LOVE. Christ demonstrated the love of God in His life and in His redeeming death on the cross. Christ's cross calls us to self-denial, nonresistance, and suffering love. God shows His love today through people who live a life of love, peace, and goodwill.

We believe that the Bible commands to love are not mere ideals, that we can't possibly live up to in this world of sin. They are imperatives to be obeyed. And we can obey them through the power God gives us. Peace is a fruit of the Spirit.

That we should love and not hate, do good for evil, and not evil for evil, is an age-old position of the Mennonite Church. Probably it is the thing we are best known for. Our peace principles are rooted in Christ and His Word. They do not stem from cowardice, an unwillingness to die, for our relief workers go into dangerous places. Neither do they come from a lack of patriotism, for we love our country and are ready to help her achieve the highest purposes of government.

WE BELIEVE that force and violence, used to enforce our will on people, are wrong. Therefore there are some things we cannot do.

We cannot harbor hatred and grudge in our hearts. The thought of hate is potential murder.

We cannot badger and threaten and bluster to get our own selfish way. Love does not seek her own advantage at the cost of another's.

We cannot try to get even with those who have treated us badly. We will seek rather to do them good, destroying enmity by kindness.

We cannot use pressure on others to secure benefits for ourselves, like higher wages.

We cannot act in ways that make people hate us and want to fight for their rights.

We cannot take part in war, because war is unchristian in its purposes, its spirit, and its method.

We cannot accept even noncombatant duty in the armed services, for every man in these services plays his part in the business of killing.

We cannot take military training.

We cannot work in munitions factories, making the guns and shells for others to shoot.

We cannot spread war propaganda, or give way to wartime hysteria.

BUT THERE ARE some things we can or must do.

We can give civilian help to the victims of war and international disorder.

We can accept a draft to alternative service which is under civilian direction.

We can make any alternative service sacrificial and a contribution to human welfare and Christian witness.

We can lead a quiet and peaceable life, in which people sense a harmony with our nonresistant stand.

We can actively help the cause of the rejected minorities, showing love to those who usually meet unconcern and hatred.

We can contribute money to help meet the needs of the hungry and the cold and the homeless; any profits which come to us because of war we can pass on to relief and rehabilitation.

We can show that we are the children of a Father who loves every race and class and nation.

For discussion:

1. How did Jesus respond to His enemies?
2. How do you know that God is love?
3. What are some things we can't do as Christian peacemakers?
4. What can we do as Christian peacemakers?

For your notebook:

Select one of the booklets in the peacemaker pamphlet series (*Why Do Men Fight? Why Be a Christian? What Does Christ Say About War? What About Church History? Is There a Middle Road? What Is Christian Citizenship?*) and write a one-page summary expressing how you feel about the pamphlet.

19. GOD ORDAINED THE STATE

We believe that the state is ordained of God to maintain order in society, and that Christians should honor rulers, be subject to authorities, witness to the state, and pray for governments.

Which of these is a Christian country: Argentina, China, Somalia, Sweden, United States?

That depends on what one means by "Christian." The official religion in Argentina is Roman Catholic, but only a small minority of the people are actively involved in the church. The country is so "unchristian" that we send missionaries there.

China is officially against all religion.

Somalia considers Islam its official religion and requires that Islam be taught in all schools.

The state church in Sweden is the Lutheran, but there is much immorality and irreligion in the country.

The United States makes a constitutional point of a strict separation between church and state. It is not a Christian country, either officially or in the quality of its life. Those of us who live here are glad for the Christian influences which have affected our country for the good. But we flinch when a Vietnamese peasant wonders why a "Christian" country drops fire on his village.

God has His "own people." But they are the church, an international body, and not any country or the people who happen to have been born and baptized there. There is a Christian church. But there is no Christian country, in which all the people believe in Christ and live by His teachings.

MOST OF US take the "free church" for granted today. But our Anabaptist fathers were doing an outlandish thing when they took their stand for the separation of church and state. For a thousand years church and state had been thought of as one, and all babies born into the states of Western Europe were baptized, and so were "Christians."

Now we members of the free churches believe that God has instituted both the church and the state. But each of these institutions has its own character and functions. The believing church, as described in the New Testament, is set off from the unbelieving world. It is a spiritual body, called to holy living in a sinning world, and to a witness to salvation through faith in Christ.

The state is the social order which God has ordained to govern the relations of all men as they live together in society. Since many of these men are of the world, and not in the church, the state is a part of the world and uses the methods of the world. It is the duty of the state to restrain evil men and to protect the law-abiding. But the state has no authority in matters of conscience and faith.

The state is responsible to God for ruling justly and providing good conditions for the lives of the citizens. Even rulers who do not acknowledge any obligation to God are nevertheless answerable to His judgment. They need to be told of the God who calls all men to repentance for evil deeds. They need to realize that the kingdoms of this world will someday become the kingdom of Christ and of God.

Members of the church are also citizens of the state. To the state they owe much: respect, honor, taxes, prayers of intercession, and obedience. The state may be disobeyed only when it asks what God forbids. But the Christian's disobedience may never be rebellion or revolution. So far as conscience allows, he must be subject even to a bad government.

THERE ARE SOME state functions in which Christians may participate, such as teaching and administration in public schools and administering health and welfare. Because the state may rely on force in administering justice, the nonresistant Christian will quickly find limits to what he can do as a part of government. Some feel that even in a democracy they should not vote. Others feel that they are responsible to get people into office who are willing to consider God's laws.

Our witness to the state can be by our words: conference statements to heads of state favoring peaceable solutions, and letters to legislators and officials, petitioning for religious freedom and civil rights. There are times for our representatives to argue in legislative hearings for righteous principles.

We do this not only to plead for our own privileges, as of conscientious objection to war, but also to express our concern for the rights of minority groups, and to protest against gambling, drinking, dirty literature in the community, and international injustice.

The church also witnesses by its own activity. Service programs of the churches gave the United States government the Peace Corps concept. Various charities of the church, like hospitals, homes, and education, have later been taken up by the state. The idea of alternative service was suggested to Congress by the church. By sacrificial service the church sets a pace that the larger society may imitate.

But the witness of the church to the state must always be in the context of announcing the gospel.

For discussion:

1. Why or why not do you feel that the United States and Canada are Christian countries?
2. What is a free church?
3. What is the purpose of government?
4. How can the church witness to the government?

For your notebook:

How do you feel about being an American or a Canadian? Write a concise statement expressing your feelings. Keep in mind both the privileges and the responsibilities of citizenship. The peacemaker pamphlet, *What Is Christian Citizenship?* provides good background.

20. CHRIST IS COMING AGAIN

We believe that at death the unsaved enter into everlasting punishment and the saved into conscious bliss with Christ, who is coming again, and will raise the dead, sit in judgment, and bring in God's everlasting kingdom.

When I was a boy, our eighth-grade arithmetic text had a section called "Thirty-three Difficult Problems." I was not very good in math, and I was stumped by a number of these problems. I might have argued that they couldn't be solved. But the answer section at the back of the book had answers for all of them. The problems that I could solve came out with a figure that I could demonstrate was correct, and that agreed with the answer in the book. The assurance that all the problems could be solved kept me working away at the tougher ones.

We live in a world that is full of problems. History

often seems to be a complicated maze, and we wonder how it will all come out. In the struggle between good and evil, who will be the victor? Will we ever realize our hopes for universal peace and joy and universal righteousness? Will evil be punished, and good be rewarded? What is there for us beyond death? Will our bodies be resurrected? Does God have His hand on history, or will it go its wild, chaotic way interminably?

These are questions for which we cannot figure out the answers. But the Bible has the answers, and we believe both the history and the prophecy of God's Word to man. For some of what was prophecy has become history. God had promised the patriarchs and the prophets of the Old Testament that He would send a Savior-Redeemer. This He did when He broke into history in Christ's incarnation, ministry, atoning death on the cross, and resurrection from the dead. In many details the prophecies were fulfilled. God made His Word good by His deeds in Christ.

Before His ascension Christ promised that He would send the Holy Spirit to guide and empower His disciples. This He did at Pentecost. Today He is working in and through His church to proclaim the gospel of salvation and to call men to turn from sin. We are living in this Spirit-age. The people of God are in conflict with the people who are against Him. This is the struggle we see going on all about us. Will this last forever?

THE BIBLE SPEAKS of this age as having an end. God will invade history again. Some of the prophecies of the Old Testament were not fulfilled in Christ's first coming. And the New Testament, which is the teaching of Christ and the apostles, is very clear in announcing a future Day of the Lord. Christ told His disciples that He was coming again. All of the writers of the New Testament present the hope of the second coming of Christ.

It is not hard to believe that Christ will come again, for that will only be an integral part of what He has already done and is doing now. Because we believe in Christ as the Son of God, we trust Him to complete the work which He began when He announced that the kingdom of God had come. Because we believe in Him as our Savior, we know that He will bring our salvation to its fulfillment in our being with Him forever. Because we have committed ourselves to Christ as our Lord, we look forward to the time when every knee shall bow to Him, when the kingdoms of this world, now far from Christian, will give way to the kingdom of our Lord Jesus Christ.

We believe that even now Christians who die depart to be with Christ. But after His coming all the dead will be raised, and Christ will be Lord of people who are completely redeemed, body and soul.

For when Christ comes again, He will exercise the judgment which the Father has given over to Him. We must all appear before Him, to give account of our attitude toward Him and of the deeds we have done. Those who are approved in that judgment will be invited to the blessedness of the eternal kingdom of God. Happy are those who will dwell forever with Christ, serving and praising Him, and exploring as they were not able to do on earth the boundless riches of His grace.

Those who are condemned in the judgment will be sent away into eternal and conscious separation from God, bearing God's wrath with the devil and his angels in the lake of fire. They consciously and responsibly rejected God's way of salvation, and now they are shut up forever to the way they have chosen. They wanted to live without God; they are sentenced to live that way forever.

HOW WILL Christ come? The Bible gives us few details. There will be a cry of command, an archangel's call, and a sound of a trumpet. He will come in the clouds, as He went away. He will come with glory and a brightness of light. How all this can be perceived worldwide we do not know. We can't even imagine it, for nothing like it has ever been in our experience.

When will He come? Of this we know still less. Aside from giving some signs, such as the preaching of the gospel to all nations, the New Testament indicates nothing about the date. We are simply told that this is something we can't and don't need to know. All we need to know is that He will certainly come. And since we don't know when, we must always be ready. For He may come at any time. We are told that many will forget and will not be watching for Him.

After He comes, then we will know how and when it was. Then we will understand many things that puzzle us now—the meaning of history, God's purpose in giving us the choice of our destiny, the nature of immortality, the celestial engineering which can raise into new and beautiful life the dust and the ashes and the decay of earth's vast graveyard.

And then we will see God's work in its consummation. Now we see that work in process; then we shall see the ends to which it has come. Then we shall rejoice that God has triumphed over all His opposers, that evil **has** been brought to an end, and that Christ shall reign **forever** and forever.

For discussion:

1. In what ways does the Bible speak of the end of this age?
2. Why is it important that Christ return?
3. How and when will Christ return?
4. How do you feel about Christ's return? Happy or sad?

For your notebook:

As a concluding project, write a 1,000 word summary of what you have gained in this study and how you feel about being a part of the Mennonite brotherhood today.

MENNONITE CONFESSION OF FAITH
Preamble

The Mennonite Church, begun in Switzerland in 1525, was a part of the Reformation which attempted to restore the New Testament church. We conceive the church to be a body of regenerated believers, a fellowship of holy pilgrims baptized upon confession of faith in Christ. As committed believers we seek to follow the way of Christian love and nonresistance, and to live separate from the evil of the world. We earnestly endeavor to make Christian disciples of all the nations.

In its beliefs the Mennonite Church is bound ultimately to the Holy Scriptures, not to any human formulation of doctrine. We regard this present confession as a restatement of the Eighteen Articles adopted at Dordrecht in the Netherlands in 1632 and of the other statements adopted by our church. In this expression of our faith we sincerely accept the lordship of Jesus Christ and the full authority of the written Word of God, the Bible, and seek to promote the unity of the brotherhood, to safeguard sound doctrine and life, and to serve as a testimony to others.

ARTICLE 1. GOD AND HIS ATTRIBUTES

We believe in almighty God, the eternal Spirit who is infinite in His attributes of holiness, love, righteousness, truth, power, goodness, and mercy. This one and only God has revealed Himself as existing eternally as Father, Son, and Holy Spirit.

The Father

We believe that God is the Creator of all things, a God of providence, and the Author of our salvation through

91

Christ. Although He is too great to be comprehended by the human mind, through Christ we can truly know Him. In redeeming love He entered into a covenant relationship with Abraham, later with the people of Israel, and has now made through Christ an eternal covenant in which He offers to the human race the forgiveness of sins and the blessings of divine sonship to those who will repent and believe.

The Son

We believe in Jesus Christ the divine Son of God, who was with the Father from all eternity, who for our salvation took upon Himself human nature, and who by His redemptive death and resurrection conquered the forces of sin and Satan and atoned for the sins of mankind. He was conceived by the Holy Spirit, born of the Virgin Mary, lived a sinless life, and in God's redemptive purpose was crucified. He rose from the dead, ascended into heaven, and now as Lord and Christ at the right hand of the Father intercedes for the saints. He is the Lord and Savior of all Christian believers and the coming judge of the living and the dead. We believe in His full deity and full humanity according to the Scriptures.

The Holy Spirit

We believe in the Holy Spirit, who was sent by the Father and the Son to bring to individuals the redemption of Christ. We believe in His personality as set forth in the Scriptures: that He loves, searches, testifies, guides, empowers, and intercedes for the saints.

Deuteronomy 6:4, 5; Matthew 22:37; John 1:18; 3:16; Romans 8:1-17; 2 Corinthians 13:14; 1 Timothy 3:16; Hebrews 11:6.

ARTICLE 2. DIVINE REVELATION

We believe that the God of creation and redemption has revealed Himself and His will for men in the Holy Scriptures, and supremely and finally in His incarnate Son, the Lord Jesus Christ. God's purpose in this revelation is the salvation of all men. Although God's power and deity are revealed in His creation, so that the nations are without excuse, this knowledge of Him cannot save men, for it cannot make Christ known. God revealed Himself in saving word and deed to Israel as recorded in the Old Testament; He fulfilled this revelation of Himself in the word and deed of Christ as recorded in the New Testament. We believe that all Scripture is given by the inspiration of God, that men moved by the Holy Spirit spoke from God. We accept the Scriptures as the authoritative Word of God, and through the Holy Spirit as the infallible Guide to lead men to faith in Christ and to guide them in the life of Christian discipleship.

We believe that the Old Testament and the New Testament together constitute the Word of God, that the Old Covenant was preparatory, that its institutions were temporary in character, and that the New Covenant in Christ is the fulfillment of the Old. We believe that the Old Testament writings are inspired and profitable, and as the divine word of promise are to be interpreted in conjunction with the divine act of fulfillment recorded in the New. Christian doctrine and practice are based upon the whole Word of God, the word of promise of the Old Covenant as fulfilled in the New.

The message of the Bible points to the Lord Jesus Christ. It is to Him that the Scriptures of the Old Testament bear witness, and He is the One whom the Scrip-

tures of the New Testament proclaim. He is the key to
the proper understanding of the entire Bible.

Psalm 19; Luke 24:27, 44; John 1:1-16; 20:31; Romans 1:19, 20; 2 Timothy 3:15, 16; Hebrews 1:1, 2; 8:6, 7; 1 John 1:1-5.

ARTICLE 3
GOD'S CREATION AND PROVIDENCE

We believe that in the beginning God created all
things by His Son, and that all existence is therefore
finite and dependent upon God, the Source and End of
all things visible and invisible. He created man in His
own image, which set man apart from the animal crea-
tion. In free will, moral character, superior intellect, and
spiritual nature, man bore the image of his Creator.

In His providence God is concerned with the lives of
His children, and in everything works for their eternal
good. He hears and answers their prayers. By Jesus
Christ He upholds the entire creation. He is Sovereign
over all things, but He is not the author of sin. He has
endowed man with the power of self-determination, and
He holds him responsible for his moral choices.

Genesis 1:1, 26, 27; Psalm 139:7-12; Matthew 10:29; John 1:3; Romans 8:28; Colossians 1:16, 17; James 5:16.

ARTICLE 4. MAN AND HIS SIN

We believe that God created man sinless and holy, and
subjected man to a moral test as a means of bringing
him to full spiritual maturity. Man yielded, however, to
the temptation of Satan and by willful disobedience to
God failed to maintain that holy condition in which he
had been created. This sin brought depravity and death
to the race. Although men are sinners by nature because
of Adam's fall, they are not guilty of his sin. Those who

94

perish eternally do so only because of their own sin. The most grievous sin is the stubborn refusal to acknowledge Jesus Christ as Savior and Lord. As a fallen creature man is self-centered, self-willed, rebellious toward God, unwilling to yield to Christ, unable to break with sin, and under divine judgment.

We believe that children are born with a nature which will manifest itself as sinful as they mature. When they come to know themselves to be responsible to God, they must repent and believe in Christ in order to be saved. Before the age when children are accountable to God, their sins are atoned for through the sacrifice of Christ. Jesus Himself assured us that children are in the kingdom of God.

Genesis 1:27, 31; 3:1-19; Matthew 18:1-14; Luke 18:16; Romans 5:12-21; Ephesians 2:1-3; 1 Timothy 4:10.

ARTICLE 5. CHRIST, THE SAVIOR FROM SIN

We believe that there is one Mediator between God and men, the Man Christ Jesus. The purpose of the incarnation of God's eternal Son was to redeem men from sin and death, to destroy the power and works of the devil, and to reconcile men to God. As a prophet, the Lord Jesus not only proclaimed God's Word; He was in His very person the Word of God. As a priest, He Himself was the sacrifice for sin, and now makes intercession with the Father for the saints. As our risen Lord and King, He is vested with all authority in heaven and on earth.

In His life the Lord Jesus demonstrated perfectly the will of God. Although tempted in all points as we are, yet He never sinned. Through the shedding of His blood He inaugurated the New Covenant, broke the pow-

95

er of sin for those who exercise faith in Him, and triumphed over Satan. By His resurrection from the dead, Christ accomplished the full justification of those who believe in Him. By faith each believer is united with the risen and glorified Christ, the Lord of glory.

Luke 19:10; John 1:1; Acts 2:33; Romans 5:11; 2 Corinthians 5:21; Colossians 2:15; 1 Timothy 2:5; Hebrews 2:14, 15; 4:15; 7:11.

ARTICLE 6
SALVATION BY GRACE THROUGH FAITH

We believe that men are saved, not by character, law, good works, or ceremonies, but by the grace of God. The merits of the death and resurrection of Christ are adequate for the salvation of all men, are offered to all, and are intended for all. Salvation is appropriated by faith in Christ. From all eternity God knew who would be the believers in Christ, and these persons foreknown as believers are elect according to the foreknowledge of God. Those who repent and believe in Christ as Savior and Lord receive the gift of righteousness, are born again, and are adopted into the family of God. Saving faith involves the giving of the self to Christ, a full surrender of the will, a confident trust in Him, a joyful obedience to His Word as a faithful disciple, and an attitude of love to all men. It is the privilege of every believer to have the assurance of salvation. The God who saves is also able to keep each believer unto a happy end in Christ. As long as the believer lives, he stands in need of the forgiveness, cleansing, and grace of Christ.

John 3:16; 10:27-29; Romans 4; Ephesians 2:8-10; 1 Peter 1:2; 1 John 1:8-10; 5:13; Jude 24.

ARTICLE 7
THE HOLY SPIRIT AND THE
CHRISTIAN LIFE

We believe that Christ as Lord and Savior does His work through the Holy Spirit. The Holy Spirit convicts of sin. Through the Holy Spirit those who believe are born again. The supreme ministry of the Spirit is to lead men to Christ and His salvation. As Christians yield to Christ and obey His Word, the Holy Spirit transforms them into the spiritual image of Jesus Christ, and enables perseverance in faith and holiness. He empowers them as effective witnesses to Christ and His salvation, fills their hearts with love for all men, and moves them to practice Christian discipleship. The Holy Spirit bestows upon each believer such gifts as He wills for the building up of the body of Christ. The indwelling of the Holy Spirit is God's seal of ownership of the Christian believer. He is God's guarantee that He will also redeem the bodies of believers on the day of Christ.

John 16:7-15; Acts 1:8; 2:1-21; 1 Corinthians 3:16, 17; 6:19; 12:11-13; chapters 12—14; Galatians 5:22-24; Ephesians 1:13, 14; 5:30.

ARTICLE 8. THE CHURCH OF CHRIST
Nature

We believe that God's redemptive work in history has led to the establishment of the Christian church. Christ established His church when He poured out His Spirit on the day of Pentecost. In preparation for this church He entered into covenant relationships with Abraham and his seed. Today the spiritual "seed of Abraham" are those who have faith in Christ, the people of God, the body of Christ, composed of believers from all races and nations. The church is the fellowship of those who are in the kingdom of Christ, the assembly of those who believe in Him, the brotherhood of the saints. The church is corporately the dwelling place of God in the Spirit, His holy temple. It is the visible body of those who are Christian disciples. Membership in the church is dependent upon a voluntary response to God's offer of salvation in Christ.

The primary unit of the church is the local assembly of believers. It is in the congregation that the work of teaching, witnessing, and disciplining is carried on. In order to maintain the unity of the church it is scriptural and profitable for congregational representatives to meet together in conferences. The concern for the welfare of the whole church calls for Spirit-led conferences to assist local congregations in maintaining biblical standards of faith, conduct, stewardship, and missions. The decisions of such conferences should be respected by the individual congregations and members.

Function

It is the function of the church to demonstrate to the world the will of God, to witness to all men of the saving power and intention of God in Christ, and to make disciples of all the nations. The church seeks to lead all men to the obedience of faith. Believers unite in the church for instruction and nurture, for worship, for inclusion in the witnessing and evangelizing body of Christ, for the observance of the ordinances, for Christian fellowship, and for the discipline of the Word and the Spirit of God. The Spirit leads the church to discover the gifts

98

which He has bestowed upon the members for the building up of the body. The church has the obligation to speak authoritatively on God's will. It shall listen to the Word of God and obey it in the moral and spiritual conflicts of each era of history.

The church is called to be a brotherhood under the lordship of Jesus Christ, a loving fellowship of brethren and sisters who are concerned for the total welfare, both spiritual and material, of one another. This concern results in the attempt to help the erring brother find the right path; it includes sharing generously both financial aid and the word of encouragement, and a willingness to give and receive counsel.

Discipline

We believe that the Lord Jesus has given authority to His church to exercise discipline. The purposes of discipline are to lead each member to full stature in Christ, to restore to full fellowship the members who fall into sin, to clarify for all members the meaning of Christian discipleship, to promote the purity of the church, to warn the weak and immature of the serious character of sin and disobedience to God's Word, and to maintain the good name and witness of the church before the world. In this work the church employs public teaching, private counseling, intercessory prayer, earnest warning and rebuke, and sympathetic encouragement. If disobedience persists, the church may withhold the right to commune until the individual repents. And the church must, with a deep sense of loss, recognize that the one who goes on to full apostasy and spiritual ruin has severed his relation with Christ and His body. The standard in church discipline is the Word of God as interpreted by the broth-

erhood. The entire congregation should share in the work of discipline and seek earnestly to win the fallen member.

Ceremonies and Practices

The Lord Jesus and His apostles instituted ordinances for the church to observe permanently as symbols of Christian truths. The Apostolic Church literally observed them. Among these are baptism with water, the communion of the Lord's Supper, the washing of the saints' feet, the holy kiss, the laying on of hands in ordination, the veiling of Christian women, the anointing of the sick with oil, and the institution of Christian marriage. When the church observes ordinances as expressions of a heart of faith, divine blessings are received, and a Christian witness is given.

Since the Lord Jesus arose from the dead on the first day of the week, the Christian church, following apostolic precedent, observes the first day of each week in memory of the Lord's resurrection.

The Church and Healing

We believe that the church should exercise a ministry of prayer for those who are in need. Prayer for the sick may be accompanied by a symbolic anointing with oil by the elders of the church. In response to the prayer of faith, and in accordance with His will, God heals in various ways, through the use of the healing arts, or by direct intervention. When healing does not occur, we believe that God's grace is sufficient. The full redemption of the body will come only at the return of Christ.

Exodus 2:24; 24:8; Matthew 5:13, 14, 23, 24; 18:15-18; 28:19, 20; Acts 15; 1 Corinthians 3:16, 17; 5:11-13; 2 Corinthians 2:6-11; 3:2; 12:9; Galatians 3:6-9; 6:1; Ephesians 2:11-22; 4:13; 1 Timothy 5:20; James 2:14-17; 5:14-16; 1 Peter 2:9.

ARTICLE 9
THE MISSION OF THE CHURCH TO SOCIETY

We believe that Christ has commissioned the church to go into all the world and make disciples of all the nations, baptizing them, and teaching them to observe His commandments. Jesus entrusted to the church the stewardship of the gospel, and promised the power of the Holy Spirit for the work of evangelism and missions. This ministry of reconciliation is inherent in the very nature of the church. The church is interested not only in the spiritual welfare of men but in their total well-being. Jesus Himself fed the hungry, healed the sick, and had compassion on the poor. The church should likewise minister to those who are in physical or social need and to those who are physically or emotionally ill. The church should witness against racial discrimination, economic injustice, and all forms of human slavery and moral degradation.

Amos 5:21-24; Matthew 28:18-20; Mark 6:56; Romans 1:16; 8:23.

ARTICLE 10. THE MINISTERS OF THE CHURCH

We believe that it is the intention of Christ that there should be shepherds in His congregations to feed the flock, to serve as leaders, to expound the Word of God, to administer the ordinances, to exercise, in cooperation with the congregation, a scriptural church discipline, and in general to function as servants of the church. Ordination is accompanied by a laying on of hands, symbolic of the church assigning responsibility and of God imparting strength for the assignment. In addition to the primary office of apostle, in the New Testament church

101

there were such gifts as prophets, evangelists, pastors, and teachers. The early church had regional overseers such as Timothy, and bishops (pastors) and deacons in the local congregations. Upon the pastors lay the responsibility for the leadership and pastoral care of the congregations, and the deacons served as their helpers. In each era of the life of the church, Christ through His Spirit seeks to lead the church to adapt its organization to the needs of time and place. The church is a brotherhood, and its organizational structure should insure the full participation of the members with their spiritual gifts in its life and discipline. It is the duty of the church to give financial support to those whom it asks to serve as evangelists, pastors, and teachers.

Matthew 23:8; 28:19; Acts 15:6; 20:28; 1 Corinthians 5:4, 5; 9:14; Ephesians 4:11, 12; Philippians 1:1; 1 Timothy 3:1-13; 4:14; 2 Timothy 4:12; Titus 1:5-9; Hebrews 13:17; 1 Peter 5:2, 3.

ARTICLE 11. CHRISTIAN BAPTISM

We believe in obeying the instruction of the Lord Jesus to baptize believers with water in the name of the Father and of the Son and of the Holy Spirit. In order to qualify for baptism one must repent, turn to Christ in sincere faith, and accept Him as Lord. We regard water baptism as an ordinance of Christ which symbolizes the baptism of the Holy Spirit, divine cleansing from sin and its guilt, identification with Christ in His death and resurrection, and the commitment to follow Him in a life of faithful discipleship. Since baptism with the Holy Spirit is a pouring out, we generally practice pouring as our mode of water baptism.

Matthew 28:18-20; Acts 2:16-21; 22:16; Romans 6:4-6; 1 Corinthians 12:13; 1 Peter 3:21.

ARTICLE 12. THE LORD'S SUPPER

We believe in observing the communion of the Lord's Supper as an ordinance instituted by Jesus Christ to symbolize the New Covenant. We recognize the bread and the cup as symbols commemorating Christ's broken body and shed blood, of our spiritual life in Him, and of the spiritual unity and fellowship of the body of Christ. Each believer shall examine himself so as not to partake of the sacred emblems carelessly or while living in sin. The church shall invite to the Lord's table only those who have peace with God and with their fellowmen, and who share the faith of the church. The Lord's Supper shall be observed faithfully until the Lord comes.

Luke 22:19, 20; 1 Corinthians 5:13; 10:16, 17; 11:24, 26.

ARTICLE 13
SYMBOLS OF CHRISTIAN BROTHERHOOD

We believe in the observance of the washing of the saints' feet as an ordinance instituted by the Lord Jesus. By His example Christ rebuked the pride and rivalry of the apostles and showed them that Christian discipleship involves obedience to His lordship and loving service. This ordinance reminds us of the brotherhood character of the church, of our mutual duty to serve and admonish one another, and of our need for continuous cleansing in our daily walk. In the New Testament the holy kiss and the right hand of fellowship are also symbols of Christian love in the church of Christ.

Luke 22:24; John 13:1-17; Romans 16:16; Galatians 2:9; 1 Timothy 5:10.

ARTICLE 14. SYMBOLS OF CHRISTIAN ORDER

We believe that in their relation to the Lord men and women are equal, for in Christ there is neither male nor female. But in the order of creation God has fitted man and woman for differing functions; man has been given a primary leadership role, while the woman is especially fitted for nurture and service. Being in Christ does not nullify these natural endowments, either in the home or in the church. The New Testament symbols of man's headship are to be his short hair and uncovered head while praying or prophesying, and the symbols of woman's role are her long hair and her veiled head. The acceptance by both men and women of the order of creation in no way limits their rightful freedom, but rather ensures their finding the respective roles in which they can most fruitfully and happily serve.

Genesis 2:18-25; 1 Corinthians 11:2-16; Galatians 3:28.

ARTICLE 15. MARRIAGE AND THE HOME

We believe that at the beginning of human history God instituted marriage. He ordained that a man shall leave his father and mother and cleave to his wife, and that the two shall become one in love and mutual submission. It is God's will that marriage be a holy state, monogamous, and for life. It is also fully acceptable to God to serve Christ unmarried. Marriage was instituted for the happiness of the husband and wife and for the procreation and Christian nurture of children. Christians shall marry only in the Lord, and for the sake of spiritual unity in the home they should become members of the same congregation. The Christian home ought regularly to have family worship, to seek faithfully to live accord-

ing to the Word of God, and to support loyally the church in its mission. We believe it is appropriate for parents to pledge themselves to the faithful Christian nurture of their children.

Genesis 1:27, 28; 2:24; Matthew 19:3-9; Mark 10:2-12; Ephesians 6:1, 4.

ARTICLE 16
DISCIPLESHIP AND NONCONFORMITY

We believe that there are two opposing kingdoms to which men give their spiritual allegiance, that of Christ and that of Satan. Those who belong to Satan's kingdom live for sin and self, and refuse the obedience of faith. The kingdom of Christ is composed of those who have been born again and who have entered into a faith union with the Lord Jesus Christ. In them the fruit of the Spirit is in evidence. They recognize the lordship of Christ, and perform all manner of good works. They seek for holiness of heart, life, and speech, and refuse any unequal yoke with unbelievers. They manifest only love toward those of other races, cultures, and economic levels. They regard their bodies as temples of the Holy Spirit and crucify their flesh with its affections and lusts. They therefore avoid such things as harmful drugs, beverage alcohol, and tobacco. We believe that their adornment should be a beauty of spirit, expressed in attire that is modest, economical, simple, and becoming to those professing Christian faith. They should seek to be Christian in their stewardship of money and possessions. Their recreational life should be consistent with the Christian walk. Through the Spirit they should put off the old man and put on the new.

Matthew 7:13, 14; Luke 9:23-26; Romans 12:1, 2; 1 Corinthians 6:12, 19; 2 Corinthians 6:14-18; Galatians 5:22-24; Ephesians 4:20-32; Colossians 1:13; 1 Timothy 2:9, 10; 1 Peter 3:3, 4.

ARTICLE 17. CHRISTIAN INTEGRITY

We believe that it is a major Christian obligation to be strictly truthful and transparent in life and doctrine, with no secrecy or hypocrisy. The Lord Jesus Christ has forbidden to His followers the use of any and all oaths, because of the finite limitations of human beings, and the obligation always to speak the truth. In legal matters we therefore simply affirm the truth. We are opposed to membership in secret societies or lodges, because such membership would involve an unequal yoke with unbelievers, and because these organizations employ hierarchical titles, require oaths, stand for organized secrecy, and may offer salvation on grounds other than faith in the Lord Jesus Christ. We believe that it is in the church that we should find love, fellowship, and security.

Matthew 5:33-37; 23:7-10, 16-22; John 18:20; Acts 4:12; 2 Corinthians 6:14—7:1; James 5:12.

ARTICLE 18. LOVE AND NONRESISTANCE

We believe that it is the will of God for His children to follow Christian love in all human relationships. Such a life of love excludes retaliation and revenge. God pours His love into the hearts of Christians so that they desire the welfare of all men. The supreme example of nonresistance is the Lord Jesus Himself. The teaching of Jesus not to resist him who is evil requires the renunciation by His disciples of all violence in human relations. Only love must be shown to all men. We believe that

106

this applies to every area of life: to personal injustice, to situations in which people commonly resort to litigation, to industrial strife, and to international tensions and wars. As nonresistant Christians we cannot serve in any office which employs the use of force. Nor can we participate in military service, or in military training, or in the voluntary financial support of war. But we must aggressively, at the risk of life itself, do whatever we can for the alleviation of human distress and suffering.

Matthew 5:38-48; John 18:36; Romans 5:5; 12:18-21; 1 Corinthians 6:1-8; 2 Corinthians 10:3, 4; James 2:8; 1 Peter 2:23; 4:1.

ARTICLE 19. THE CHRISTIAN AND THE STATE

We believe that the state is ordained of God to maintain law and order. We seek to obey the New Testament commands to render honor to the authorities, to pay our taxes, to obey all laws which do not conflict with the higher law of God, and to pray for our rulers. The church should also witness to the authorities of God's redeeming love in Christ, and of His sovereignty over all men. In law enforcement the state does not and cannot operate on the nonresistant principles of Christ's kingdom. Therefore, nonresistant Christians cannot undertake any service in the state or in society which would violate the principles of love and holiness as taught by Christ and His inspired apostles.

Acts 4:19; 5:29; Romans 13:1-7; Ephesians 1:20-22; 5:23; 1 Timothy 2:1, 2.

ARTICLE 20. THE FINAL CONSUMMATION

We believe that in addition to the physical order with which our senses are related, there also exists an eternal spiritual order, the realm of God, of Christ, of the Holy Spirit, of the angels, and of the church triumphant. We believe that at death the righteous enter at once into conscious joy and fellowship with Christ, while the wicked are in a state of conscious suffering. The church militant lives and witnesses in this present evil world, a world in which apostasy from God is to become even more pronounced. The church also looks forward with hope to the day of the Lord, to the personal return of Christ, and the glorious future of the kingdom of God. In His triumphant second coming Christ will judge Satan, and usher in the consummation of all things. His coming will introduce the resurrection, the transformation of the living saints, the judgment of the just and the unjust, and the fulfillment of His glorious reign. He will deliver the kingdom to God the Father, cleanse the world by fire, create new heavens and a new earth, consign unbelievers to eternal punishment, and usher His children into the eternal bliss of the world to come.

Daniel 12:2; Matthew 25:34, 41; Mark 9:43-48; Luke 16:22, 23; John 5:22; 1 Corinthians 15:24, 35-58; 2 Corinthians 5:1-4; Philippians 1:23; 1 Thessalonians 4:13—5:4; 1 Peter 1:4; 2 Peter 3:3-13; Revelation 15:3; 21:4; 22:3.

May God enable us all to attain His eternal kingdom prepared for us from the foundation of the world, that with His blessed Son we may enjoy fullness of life for ever and ever.

For Additional Study

The following booklets are suggested for additional study or reading:

Peacemaker Pamphlets

Hurt in the Heart by Urie A. Bender

Alcohol and Your Life by Loren Lind and Willard Krabill, MD

Tobacco and Your Life by Loren Lind and Willard Krabill, MD

Your Body and You by Lois and Arthur Kennel, MD

After High School—What? by Atlee Beechy

The Author

Paul Erb was born in Kansas in 1894, the son of T. M. Erb, pioneer of the Mennonite churches of the West, and one of the founders of Hesston College. He has been a teacher, preacher, editor, writer, promoter of missions, and churchman in general.

He was executive secretary of Mennonite General Conference at the time of the adoption of the 1963 Confession of Faith, and had a part in its writing.

He initiated the planning for and gave early direction to Mennonite Youth Fellowship, which was an important stage in the development of a youth program for the Mennonite Church.

He was editor for eighteen years of the *Gospel Herald,* official organ of the Mennonite Church.

Earlier publications have been *What It Means to Be a Mennonite, Old Testament Poetry and Prophecy, The Alpha and the Omega* (Conrad Grebel Lectures), *Don't Park Here,* and *Our Neighbors South and North.* He was chairman of the Publishing Committee for the *Mennonite Encyclopedia,* and he edited *From the Mennonite Pulpit.*

He married Alta Mae Eby, teacher and writer. Their children are Winifred Erb Paul and J. Delbert Erb.

He lives at Scottdale, Pennsylvania, and serves the Allegheny Mennonite Conference as field worker.